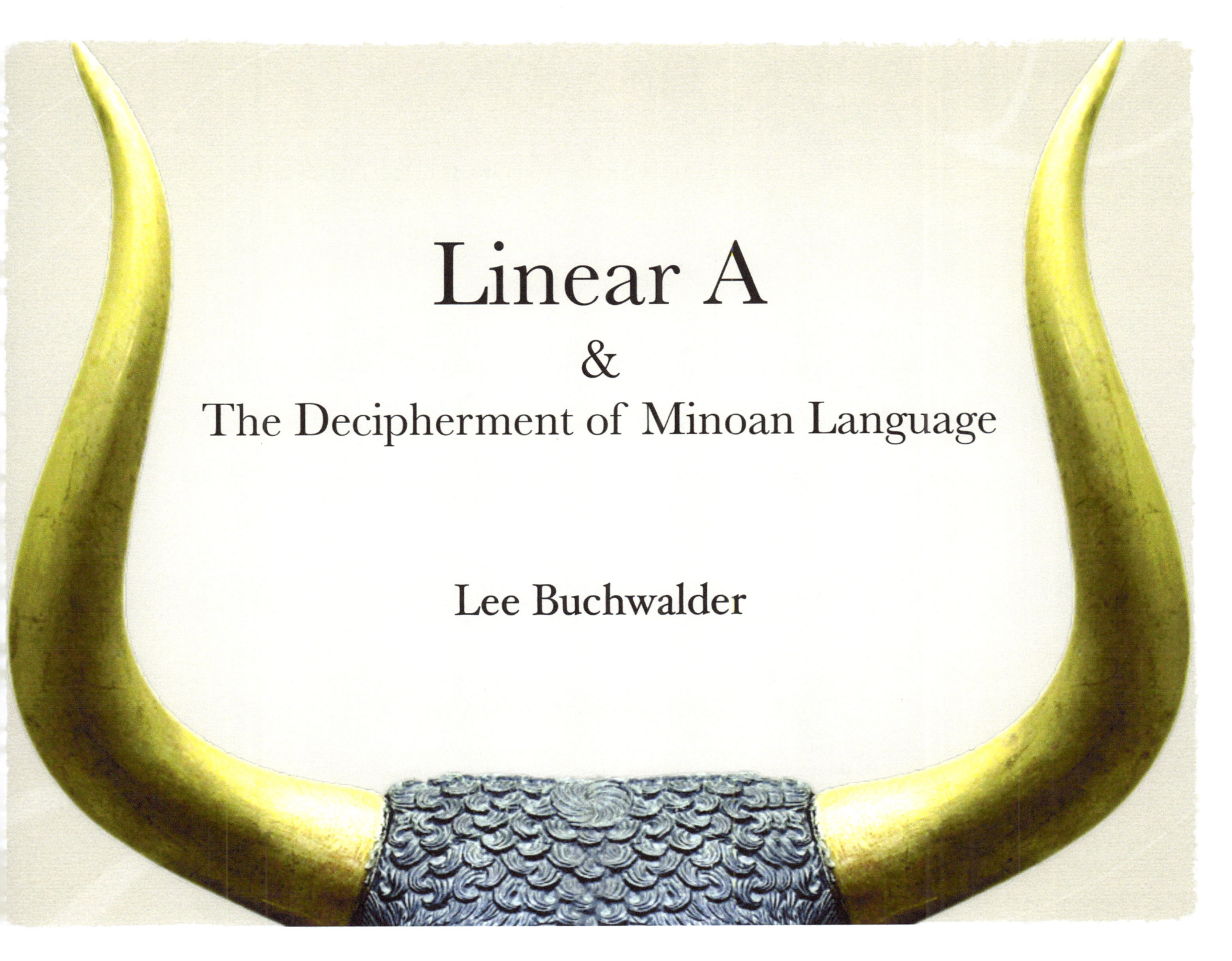

Linear A
&
The Decipherment of Minoan Language

Lee Buchwalder

Linear A
& The Decipherment of Minoan Language

Branch Publishing LLC
New York

www.BranchPublishingLLC.com

Copyright © 2019 Lee Buchwalder

First Edition 2020

All rights reserved. No part of this book may be reproduced, stored in a retrieval system or transmitted in any form or by any means electronic, mechanical, photocopying, recording, or otherwise without prior written permission from the publisher.

Cover design: Lee Buchwalder
Artifact illustrations: Chris Fowler
Reconstruction of a Minoan wall painting from Akrotiri: Balage Balogh
Photograph of the Priest-King fresco (https://commons.m.wikimedia.org/wiki/File:Knossos_frise2.JPG): Harrieta171 © 2006; Edited by Lee Buchwalder. CC License (CC BY-SA 3.0); https://creativecommons.org/licenses/by-sa/3.0/legalcode
Photograph of a bull's-head rhyton from Knossos: John Copland/Shutterstock.com
Labyrinth vector: George J/Shutterstock.com

Publisher's Cataloging-In-Publication Data (Prepared by The Donohue Group, Inc.)

Names: Buchwalder, Lee, author.
Title: Linear A & the decipherment of Minoan language / Lee Buchwalder.
Other Titles: Linear A and the decipherment of Minoan language
Description: First Edition. | New York : Branch Publishing, 2020. | Includes bibliographical references.
Identifiers: ISBN 9781735187402 (hardcover) | ISBN 9781735187419 (paperback)
Subjects: LCSH: Inscriptions, Linear A. | BISAC: FOREIGN LANGUAGE STUDY / Ancient Languages. | LANGUAGE ARTS & DISCIPLINES / Alphabets & Writing Systems. | LANGUAGE ARTS & DISCIPLINES / Linguistics / General. | LANGUAGE ARTS & DISCIPLINES / Linguistics / Etymology.
Classification: LCC P1037 .B834 2020 | DDC 410–dc23

Library of Congress Control Number: 2020910433

光日キ

Contents

Linear A Inscriptions	6
Premise	7
1. Methodology	9
2. Alphabetic Conversion	27
3. Affixes	33
4. The Ritual Sequence	37
5. Vocabulary	47
6. Artifact Translations	51
Summary	83
References	84

Linear A Inscriptions

Phonetic transcriptions by John Younger (Younger 2020: LinearA/)[1] based on Godart and Olivier (GORILA 1976–1985: vol. I–V).[2]

ARKH Zf 9 (YJG), silver hairpin JA-KI-SI-KI-NU • MI-DA-MA-RA$_2$ • [1]

CR Zf 1 (GORILA IV: 146-147, 162) (YJG), gold pin (cf. KN Zf 1) A-MA-WA-SI • KA-NI-JA-MI • I-JA • QA-KI-SE-NU-TI • A-TA-DE [1][2]

HT 41 (YJG), tablet (excerpt) MI-DA-NI • PA-JA [1]

HT 154A (YJG), tablet (excerpt) TU-ME-PA-JA[[1]

IO Za 2&11 (GORILA V: 18-19) (YJG), ritual tables : (excerpt)]U-TI-NU • I-NA-I-DA-•[[1]
  A-TA-I-*301-WA-JA • JA-DI-KI-TU • JA-SA-SA-RA[-ME • U-NA-KA-NA-]SI [•] I-PI-NA-MA • SI-RU-TE • TA-NA-RA-TE-U-TI-NU • I-•-•[[1][2]

IO Za 5 (GORILA V: 22-23) (YJG), lamp]I-JA-RE-DI-JA • I-JA-PA[[1][2]

IO Za 6 (GORILA V: 24-27) (YJG), dish TA-NA-I-*301-U-TI-NU • I-NA-TA-I-ZU-DI-SI-KA • JA-SA-SA-RA-ME • [1][2]

IO Za 8 (GORILA V: 30-31) (YJG), ritual table] A-NA-TI-*301-WA-JA [[1][2]

KE Zb 4 (GORILA IV: 72) (YJG), lamp • JA-SI-E [1][2]

KN Za 10 (GORILA IV: 8-9) (YJG), ritual table]-TA-NU-MU-TI • JA-SA-SA-RA-MA-NA • DA-WA-[•]-DU-WA-TO • I-JA[[1][2]

KN Zc 6 (GORILA IV: 118-121) (YJG), cup with painted inscription *34-TI-RI A-DI-DA-KI-TI-PA-KU • NI-JA-NU • JU-KU-NA-PA-KU-NU-U[-•]-I-ZU • [1][2]

KN Zc 7 (GORILA IV: 122-125) (YJG), cup A-KA-NU-ZA-TI • DU-RA-RE • A-ZU-RA • JA-SA-RA-A-NA-NE • WI-PI-[•] [1][2]

KN Ze 44 (YJG), inscription I-A301?-WA-JA [1]

KN Zf 13 (GORILA IV: 152-153, 162) (YJG), gold ring A-RE-NE-SI-DI-*301-PI-KE-PA-JA-TA-RI-SE-TE-RI-MU-A-JA-KU [1][2]

KN Zf 31 (GORILA IV: 154-155, 162) (YJG), silver pin :
  ]SI[ ]SI-ZA-NE-*310 • DA-DU-MI-NE • QA-MI-*47-NA-RA • A-WA-PI • TE-SU-DE-SE-KE-I • A-DA-RA • TI-DI-TE-QA-TI • TA-SA-ZA • TA-TE-I-KE-ZA-RE •[[1][2]

KO Za 1 (GORILA IV: 18-20) (YJG), stone base A-TA-I-*301-WA-JA TU-RU-SA • DU-PU$_3$-RE • I-DA-A • U-NA-KA-NA-SI • I-PI-NA-MA • SI-RU-TE [1][2]

KO Zf 2 (GORILA IV: 158-159) (YJG), bowl A-RA-KO-KU-ZU-WA-SA-TO-MA-RO-AU-TA-DE-PO-NI-ZA [1][2]

PE Zb 7 (YJG), pithos]-A JA-WA-PI 1 [1]

PH 6 (GORILA I: 292-3) (YJG), tablet I-NA-WA • A-RI I-ZU-RI-NI-TA A-RI I-DA-PA$_3$-I-SA-RI [1][2]

PH Zb 5 (GORILA IV: 94) (YJG), pithos WA-PI-TI-NA-RA$_2$ [1][2]   NA[2]

PK Za 8 (GORILA IV: 24-27) (YJG notes the text TU-ME-I   ]-NU • PA$_3$-E • JA-DI-KI-TE-TE-*307-PU$_2$-RE • TU-ME-I JA-SA-[ ] U-NA-KA-NA-SI[ ] I-PI-[[1][2]
  occurring on **PK Za 8a** also), ritual table

PK Za 11 (GORILA IV: 32-34) (YJG finds the text A-DI-KI-TE-TE-   A-TA-I-*301-WA-E • A-DI-KI-TE-TE-[••]-RE • PI-TE-RI • A-KO-A-NE • A-SA-SA-RA-ME •
  DU-PU-RE and SI-RU-TE more probable), ritual table   U-NA-RU-KA-NA-TI • I-PI-NA-MI-NA[ ] SI-RU-[•] • I-NA-JA-PA-QA [1][2]

PK Za 12 (GORILA IV: 35-38) (YJG), ritual table (excerpt) • U-NA-RU-KA[1?]JA-SI • [1][2]

PK Za 14 (GORILA IV: 39-40) (YJG), ritual table -TU-ME-I • JA-SA-SA-[[1][2]

PK Za 16 (GORILA IV: 42) (YJG), ritual table]-TO-SA • PU$_2$-RE-JA[ ]vest.[[1][2]

PR Za 1 (GORILA IV: 46-49) (YJG), chest TA-NA-SU-TE[ ]-KE SE-TO-I-JA A-SA-SA-RA-ME [1][2]

PS Za 2 (YJG), ritual table (excerpt) TA-NA-I-*301-TI • [1]

SKO Zc 1 (YJG), fragments of a chalice rim (fragment 1)]vest. • NA-TU-*301-NE[[1]

TL Za 1 (GORILA IV: 58-59) (YJG), ladle A-TA-I-*301-WA-JA • O-SU-QA-RE • JA-SA-SA-RA-ME • U-NA-KA-NA-[SI I-PI]-NA-MA SI-RU-[TE [1][2]

ZA Zb 3 (GORILA IV: 112-113) (YJG), pithos (excerpt) VINa 32 DI-DI-KA-SE • A-SA-MU-NE • [1][2]

ZA Zg 35 (YJG), bone label]ME-MI-JA-RU • SE-WA-AU-DE [1]

Premise

Proto-Indo-European vocabulary is known to contain root words that are reflected in later languages: most notably Latin, Greek, German, and English. By examining parallel sentence structures in the undeciphered script known as Linear A, it is possible to demonstrate that its language is Proto-Indo-European in origin. These parallels are seen to occur as unique synonym couplings, some of which have even survived into modern English. Therefore, lexical analysis of a language closely related to that of Linear A can often reduce the range of possible meanings for each of these pairs to a single one. That may come as a surprise to many linguists. But what is even more surprising is that the vowels in a parallel are often irrelevant, and the identical result is obtained regardless of their values. Debate over their varying pronunciations in the ancient past is thus rendered moot. In other words, consonant-parallels alone are capable of reducing the number of matching synonym pairs within the entire vocabulary of a given language to just one. If a string of these parallels, as they occur in Linear A, should thereby produce intelligible sentences, then a definite relationship between languages has been demonstrated. With the vocabulary deciphered, occasional vowel conflicts with linguistic reconstructions can be assessed and are posited to be the result of orthographic changes that arrived with the development of Linear B.

8

1. Methodology

Methodology

Due to the use of parallel vocabulary on Minoan artifacts,
it is possible to correlate Linear A with European languages.

Examples of Parallel Phrases in Linear A

(Phonetic values of the symbols are known from Linear B.)

1. / U-NA-RU-KA-JA-SI /

2. JA-SA-SA-RA-ME / U-NA-RU-KA-NA-TI / I-PI-NA-MI-NA / SI-RU-TE

3. A-SA-SA-RA-ME / U-NA-KA-NA-SI / I-PI-NA-MA / SI-RU-TE

4. A-SA-MU-NE /

Using Parallelism to Identify Compound Words

Compound words can be identified by a divergence in parallel symmetry between two or more examples. This frequently involves a consonant change.

1. / U-NA-RU-KA-JA-SI /

2. JA-SA-SA-RA-ME / U-NA-RU-KA-NA-TI / I-PI-NA-MI-NA / SI-RU-TE

3. A-SA-SA-RA-ME / U-NA-KA-NA-SI / I-PI-NA-MA / SI-RU-TE

4. A-SA-MU-NE /

These words are similar but not identical. This suggests that they are conceptually related.

The text on the artifact in example one is not entirely clear. It may contain either a space or an extra syllable. A synonym parallel, discussed later on, assists in defining this word-break.

Methodology

The key to deciphering Linear A is understanding the deep significance of the differences that occur when a single concept is expressed multiple ways.

Parallel Variation

+ j / - j   sar / mun   + ru / - ru   t / s   + na / - na

1. JA-SA / SA-RA-ME / U-NA-RU-KA / NA-TI / I-PI-NA-MI-NA / SI-RU-TE
2. A-SA / SA-RA-ME / U-NA-KA / NA-SI / I-PI-NA-MA / SI-RU-TE
3. A-SA / MU-NE /

▓ = significant variation which can be compared with Latin and English to determine the meaning of a pair of analogous words with certainty.

Parallel Variation Analysis

The root pairs listed below are from a sequence of parallels in Linear A. They can be deciphered by comparison with Latin and English lexicons, based on the assumption that their parallel usage implies synonymous meaning. The pages which follow illustrate that the requirement for parallel roots to be synonymous often limits the results to a single synonym pair in Latin or English. If a string of these parallels, as they occur in Linear A, should thereby produce meaningful phrases, then a definite relationship with these later languages has been demonstrated. Vowel changes in some of the roots are known to have occurred since the time that Linear A was in use and will be discussed in an upcoming chapter. However, in the following analysis they are irrelevant because consonant-parallels are seen to be effective in bypassing such vowel changes entirely.

1. NAT / NAS
2. SAR / MUN
3. NAM / NAMIN + (IPINAM)
4. JAS / AS
5. UNARK / UNK

NAT / NAS Parallel Root Analysis (English)

An assessment of the total number of NAT / NAS based synonym pairs within a 350,000 word English lexicon.[3]

NAT (130 words) | NAS (40 words)

Nation (44) — a group of people **born** in the same region or of common ancestry. Ultimately from Latin root meaning born.

Native (13) — a person **born** in a particular area. Ultimately from Latin root meaning born.

Nature (46) — from Latin natura: **birth** or the natural order. Ultimately from Latin root meaning born.

Natal (2) — relating to **birth**. Ultimately from Latin root meaning born.

Nascent (3) — being **born**. Ultimately from Latin root meaning born.

Nast - (5) — related to nasty.

Nas - (2) — science, plant, animal, and anatomy words.

Natat - (5) — related to swimming.

Nat - (7) — science, plant, animal, anatomy words, and a contraction.

Natty (4) — altered forms of neat and notty.

Natter (2) — to talk with little substance.

Nat - (7) — proper nouns unrelated to other NAT entries.

Nasal - (10) — related to nose.

Nas - (20) — proper nouns unrelated to other NAS entries.

105/130
approximately 80 percent of English NAT words are related to **birth**.

3/40 or (**3/20** without proper nouns)
approximately 15 percent of English NAS words are related to being **born**.

Total number of synonym pairs in the English language which begin with the letter groups NAT and NAS =
1 (birth / born)

NAT / NAS Parallel Root Analysis (Latin)

An assessment of the total number of NAT / NAS based synonym pairs within a standard Latin lexicon.[4]

NAT (12 words) | NAS (7 words)

Natio (1)
birth. Also a group of people born in the same region or of common ancestry.

Nativus (1)
native, born or innate.

Natura - (3)
birth or the natural order.

Natal - (2)
relating to birth.

Nascor (1)
to be born.

Nassa (1)
a trap or basket.

Nas - (1)
science, plant, animal, and anatomy words.

Nat - (3)
related to swimming.

Nat - (2)
science, plant, animal, and anatomy words.

Nas - (2)
related to nose.

Nas - (2)
proper nouns unrelated to other NAS entries.

7/12
approximately 60 percent of Latin NAT words are related to **birth**.

1/7 or (1/5 without proper nouns)
approximately 20 percent of Latin NAS words are related to being **born**.

Total number of synonym pairs in Latin
which begin with the letter groups
NAT and NAS =
1 (birth / born)

NA-TI / NA-SI

The relationship between natal and nascent as reflected in the parallel vocabulary of Latin and Linear A.

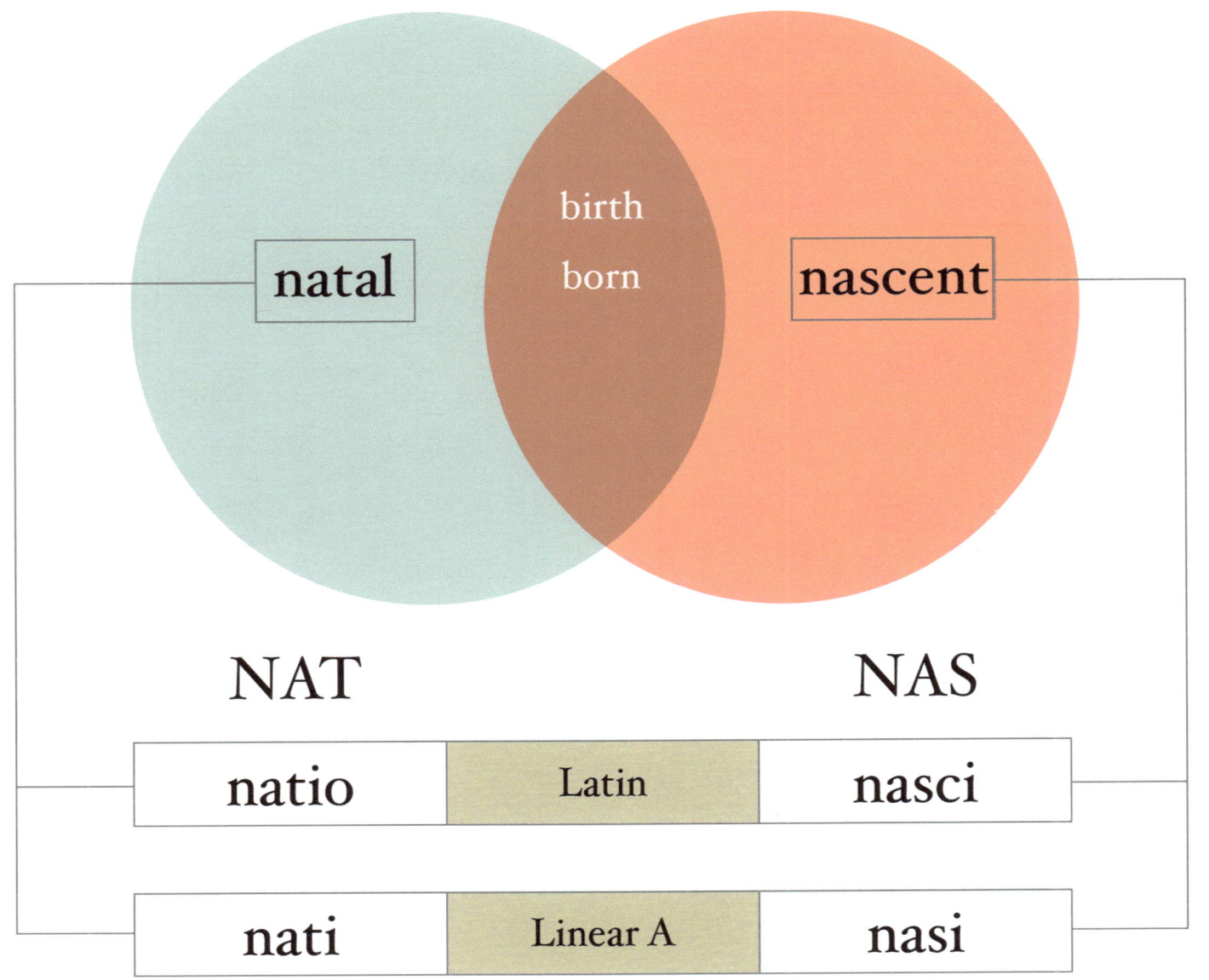

SAR / MUN Parallel Root Analysis (Latin)

An assessment of the total number of SAR / MUN based synonym pairs within a standard Latin lexicon.[4]

SAR (19 words) | MUN (20 words)

Sartus / Sarcio (3)
patch, mend, to make amends. Also a cobbler.

Sarcina (3)
burden, load, or sorrow.

Sarrio / Sarculum (2)
to hoe or weed.

Sarmentum (1)
twigs.

Sarcophagus (1)
a coffin.

Mund - (2)
earth, world.

Munim - (5)
protection and fortification.

Mund - (2)
clean or neat.

Mun - (3)
towns and municipalities.

Sar - (3)
Sardis, Sardinia and Sarmatia. Place names.

Sard - (1)
name of stone.

Sarracum (1)
wagon or cart.

Sartago (1)
mixture. Also a frying pan

Sar - (3)
related to fish.

Mun - (7)
duty. Also official functions / giving and offering.

Mun - (1)
proper nouns unrelated to other NAS entries.

3/19

approximately 15 percent of Latin SAR words are related to **burden**.

7/20

approximately 35 percent of Latin MUN words are related to **duty**.

Total number of synonym pairs in Latin
which begin with the letter groups
SAR and MUN =
1 (burden / duty)

SA-RA / MU-NE

The relationship between burden and duty as reflected in the parallel vocabulary of Latin and Linear A.

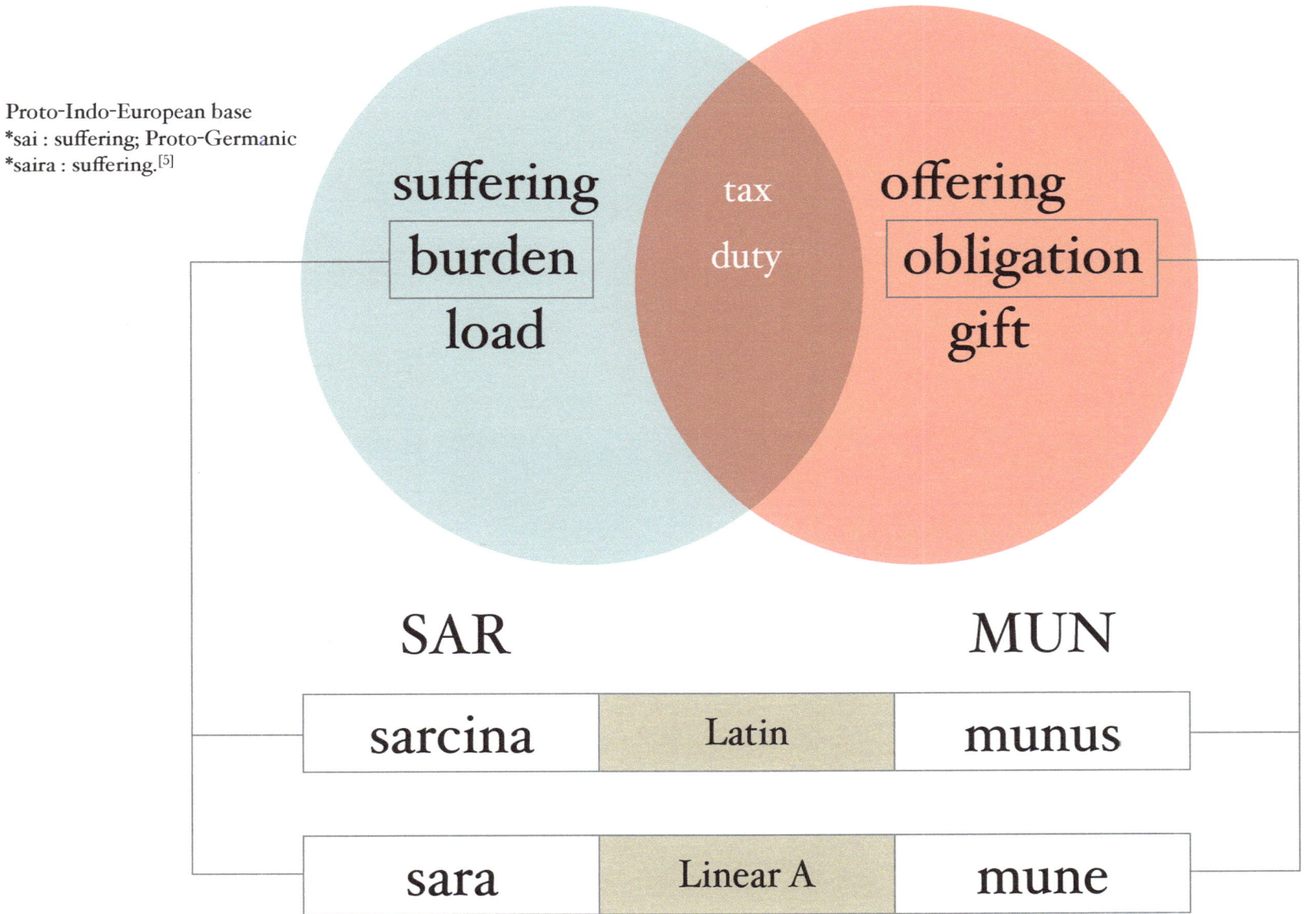

Proto-Indo-European base
*sai : suffering; Proto-Germanic
*saira : suffering.[5]

NAM/NAMIN Parallel Root Analysis (English)

An assessment of the total number of N-(vowel)-M / N-(vowel)-M-(vowel)-N based synonym pairs within a 350,000 word English lexicon.[3]

N-(vowel)-M (130 words)

Name (17)

name.

Nam - (16)

namaskar - 1.
namaste - 1.
namby-pamby - 1.
nam - (proper nouns) - 13.

Nem - (19)

nemesis - 2.
nem - (science etc.) - 17.

Nim - (10)

nim (game) - 1.
nimble - 3.
nimbus - 2.
nimrod - 1.
nim - (proper nouns) - 3.

Nom - (20)

nom - (law / science) - 9.
nomad - 4.
no-man - 1.
nomarchy - 1.
nombril - 1.
nom-de- (pseudonym) - 2.
nom - (proper nouns) - 2.

Num - (48)

numb - 6.
number / numer - 35.
numbles - (entrails) - 1.
numdah - (rug) - 1.
num - (science etc.) - 2.
num - (proper nouns) - 3.

17/130

approximately 13 percent of English N-(vowel)-M words are related to **name**.

N-(vowel)-M-(vowel)-N (30 words)

Nam-n (1)

naming.

Nam-n / Nem-n (4)

proper nouns.

Nim-n (1)

niminy-piminy.

Nom-n (21)

nomen-/nomin-.
Latin root
meaning name.

Num-n (3)

numen - (spirit).

22/30 or **(22/26** without proper nouns **)**

approximately 85 percent of English N-(vowel)-M-(vowel)-N words are related to **name**.

Total number of synonym pairs in the English language which begin with the letter groups
N-(vowel)-M and N-(vowel)-M-(vowel)-N =
1 (name / nomen- or nomin-)

NA-MA / NA-MI-NA

The relationship between name and nomen as reflected in the parallel vocabulary of Greek, Latin, and Linear A.

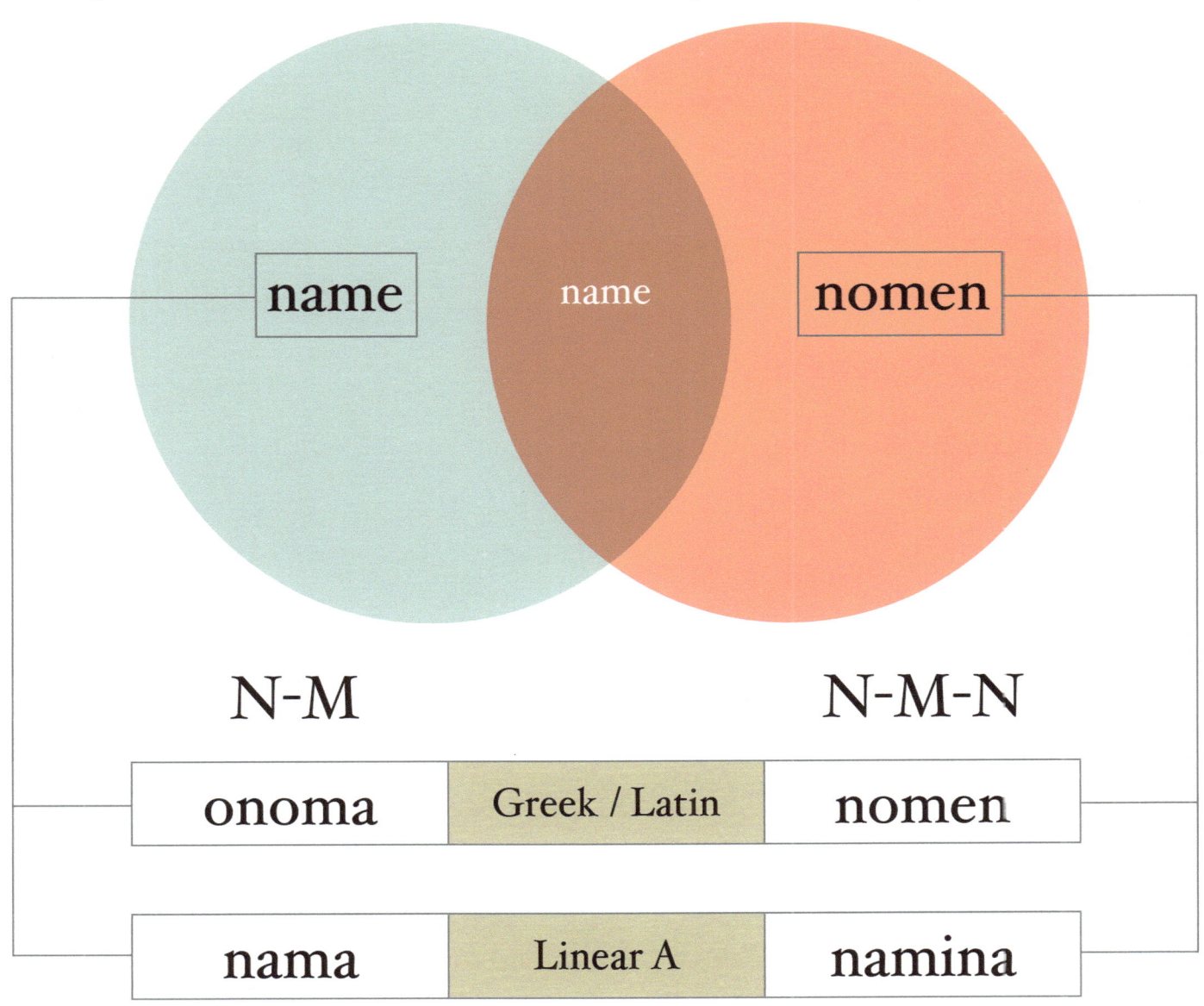

JAS / AS Parallel Root Analysis (Latin)

An assessment of the total number of I-(vowel)-S / (vowel)-S based synonym pairs within a standard Latin lexicon.[4]

I-(vowel)-S (10 words) | (vowel)-S (110 words)

Ias - (2)   Ies - (0)   Iis - (0)   Ios - (0)   Ius - (1)   As - (50)   Es - (10)

Jason. Jasper.

broth or soup.

Is - (10)   Os - (30)   Us - (5)

words unrelated to the next entry.

The JASA / ASA parallel in Linear A should become IASA / ASA in Latin, which uses the letter I rather than J. Given that there are only two words in Latin which begin with IAS, both of which are contextually irrelevant, a vowel shift is suspected. Substituting U for A forms the Latin roots **IUS** and **US**. This yields compelling results which suggest that the Latin parallel iussu / usu originated from JASA / ASA in Linear A and that they are, in fact, the same pair of words. See diagram on the next page.

Ius - (7)

relating to **Jus**-tice, **law**, and **order**.

Us - (5)

use, **custom** or application.

7/10

approximately 70 percent of Latin I-(vowel)-S words are related to **Jus**-tice, **law**, and **order**.

5/110

approximately 5 percent of Latin (vowel)-S words are related to **custom**.

Total number of synonym pairs in Latin which begin with the letter groups IUS and US (or any parallel vowel substitute) = 1 (law / custom)

JA-SA / A-SA

The relationship between law and custom as reflected in the parallel vocabulary of Latin and Linear A.

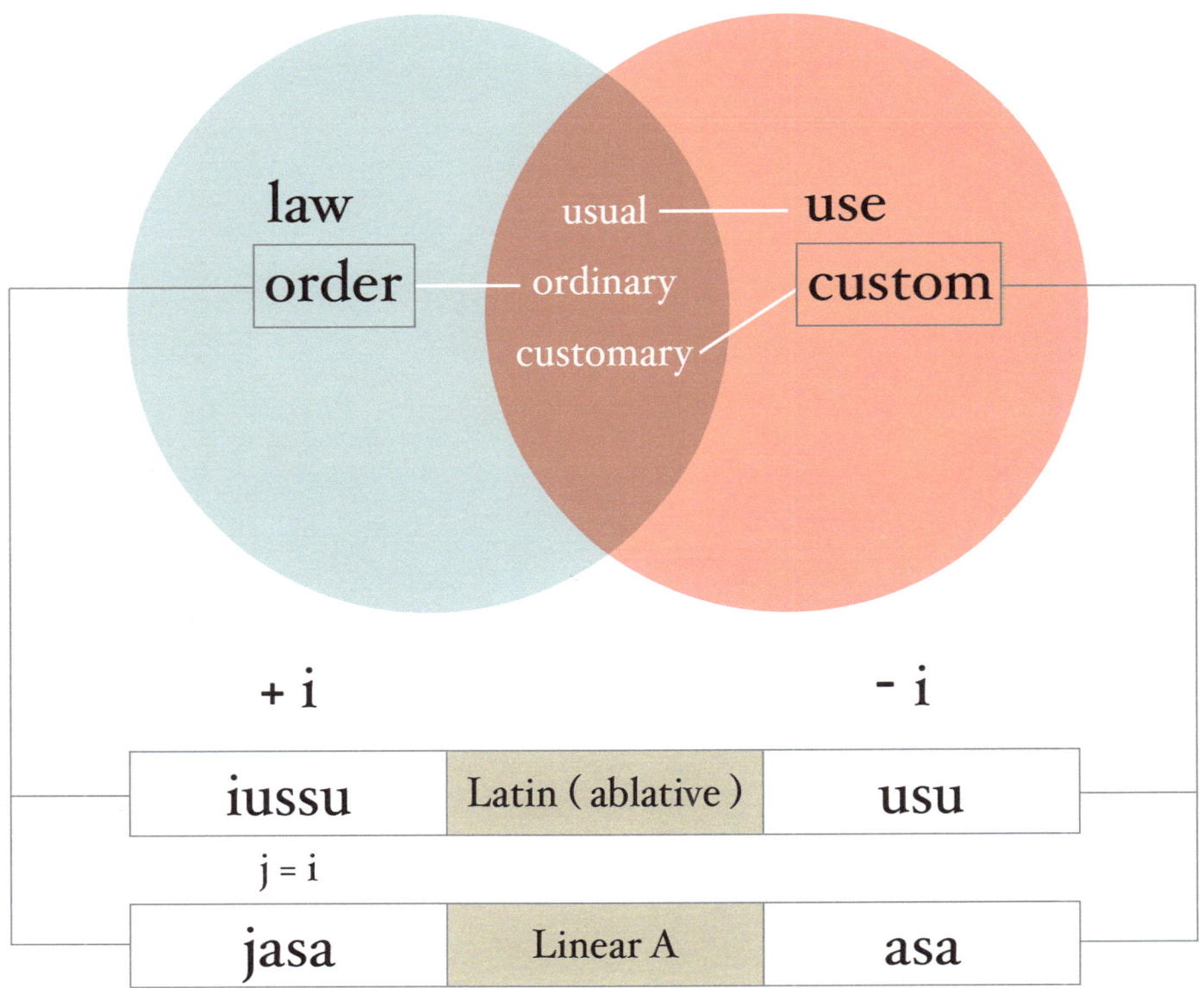

The parallel usage of JASA / ASA in Linear A reveals the same relationship between **iussu** and **usu** in Latin. By removing the initial letter of the first word in each language, a synonym is produced. This strongly suggests that Linear A is the source of this previously unknown relationship in Latin. Additionally, the central section of the diagram illustrates the mutual tendency of these words to mean that which is **normal**. This is probably because law and **order** often determine common social practices and **customs**.

U-NA-RU-KA / U-NA-KA

The relationship between arch and hook as reflected in the parallel vocabulary of Greek, Latin, and Linear A.

In Greek and Latin, the word arkhos / arcus has divergent meanings (chief / arc). Both senses appear to have been previously united in Linear A.

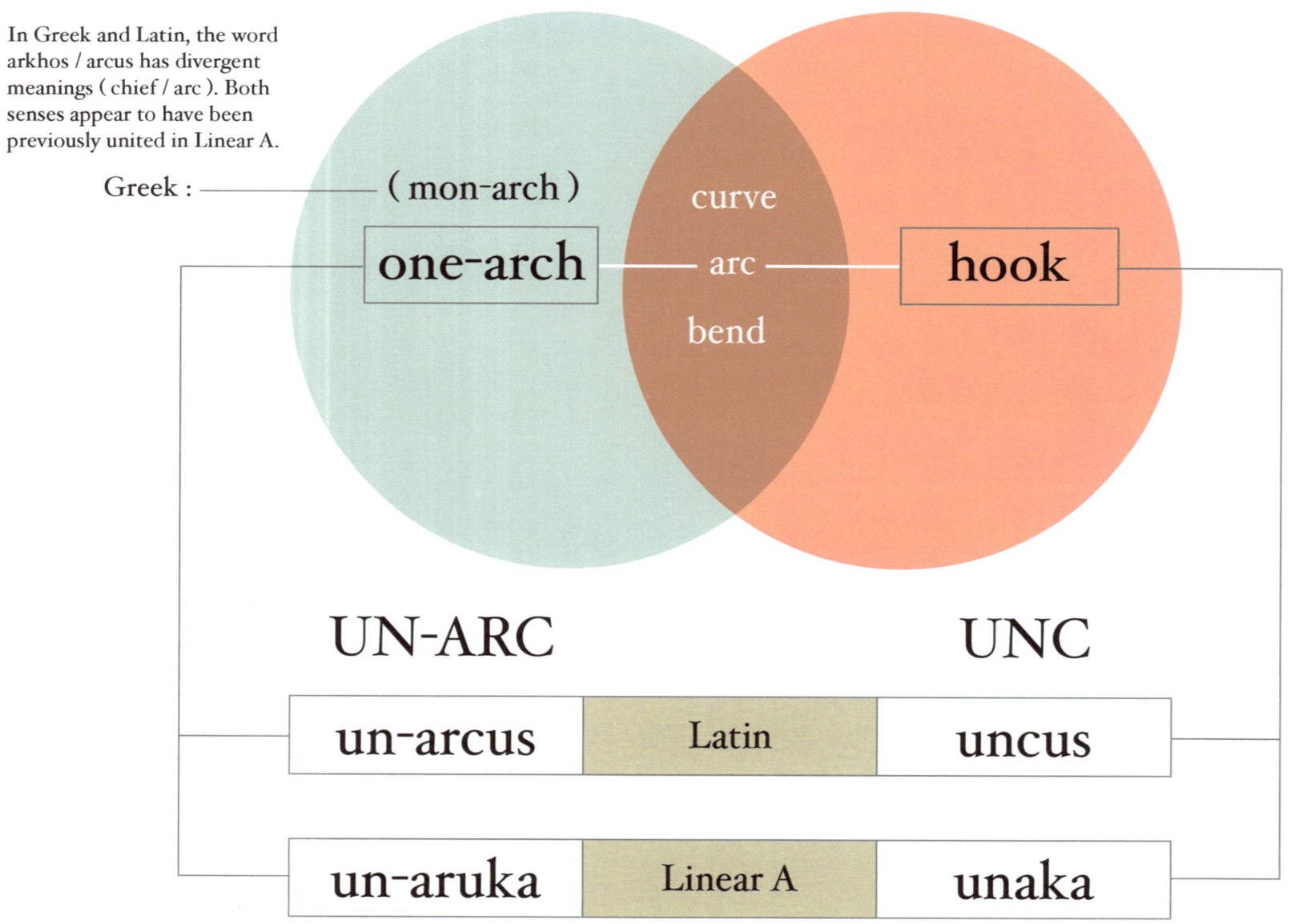

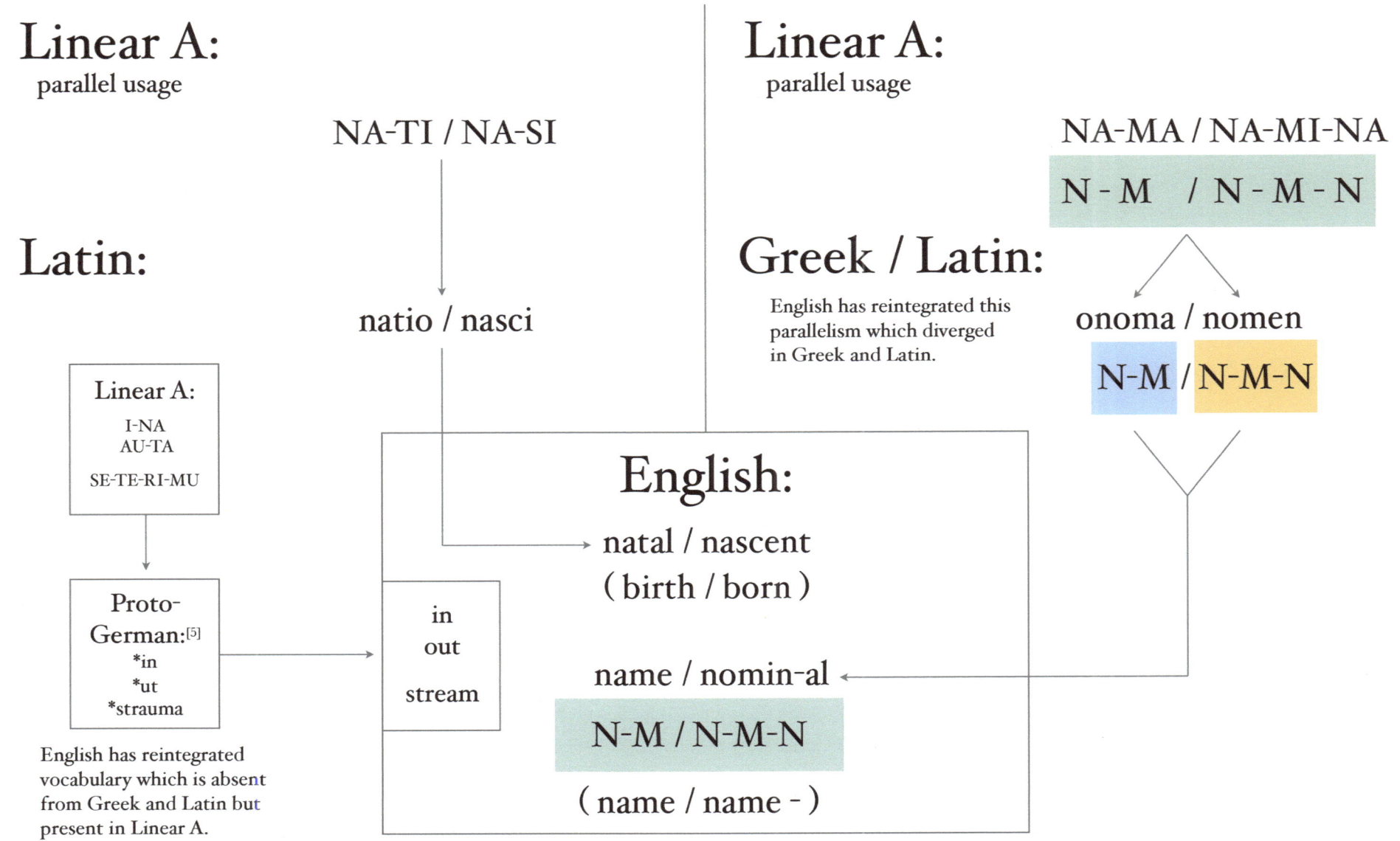

Methodology (In Context)

Compound words are identified and divided by marking a divergence in parallel symmetry.

A-SA-SA-RA = ⌈ A-SA-SA-RA
A-SA-MU-NE   ⌊ A-SA-MU-NE

This process often yields root words with parallel meanings. In this case, **burden / duty**.

(ablative)

(j = i in Latin)

(+ i) JA-SA = Latin **iussu** = **jus**-tice / law / → by Ord-er of Duty

(− i) A-SA = Latin **usu** = **use** / custom /

⌊ JA-SA-SA-RA

This word division is based on a parallel with the example above. The words are also divided this way on bifacial Minoan seals. JA-SA and A-SA are analogous. Their parallel usage provides a hint that the discrepancy in their first syllables is the key to identifying these words in Latin.

U-NA-RU-KA-JA-SI   U-NA-RU-KA-JA-SI
U-NA-RU-KA-NA-TI   =   U-NA-RU-KA-NA-TI
U-NA-KA-NA-SI   U-NA-KA-NA-SI

The text is not entirely clear on this artifact. (NA)-JA-SI is also possible.[1] If that is correct, it may be a known variant of NA-SI. The synonyms help determine this word-break. See page 50.

Related Latin roots meaning **birth** and **born**. These relate to the king's authority by birth. (the born-king)

These are synonymous words meaning king. U-NA-RU-KA is a Latinized form of the Greek based **monarch** (one + arch) or **one + highest / chief**. (un / unus in Latin being equivalent to mon / monos in Greek). The letter U in RU may initially seem puzzling, but all Linear A consonants require a vowel after them. This coupling is not required in the Latin alphabet. The word U-NA-KA resembles Linear B wanaka, meaning king. The letters U and W produce similar sounds.

Methodology (In Context)

English: (- P - N - M)

Linear A: I-PI-NA-MA
I-PI-NA-MI-NA

Only a single word in the English language matches the letter profile vowel P vowel N vowel M, and that is the word **eponym**. (from Greek epi + onoma / upon + name)[6]

Having divided the compound word in this manner, a parallel is discovered based on the Linear A variants N-M and N-M-N.

The consonant parallel N-M / N-M-N is only shared between words with one root meaning in English (name). The words **name** and **nomin**-al are an example of this relationship.

SI-RU-TE

No specific parallel variant can be found for this word. However, given the context of the sentence and the close relationship between Linear A and Latin, it is almost certain that the word means **sire** (seior in Latin). Based on other examples, the syllable TE may be an affix meaning **a** or **the**. Its unusual placement after the noun may be in response to an indefinite article in the word **un**-arc.

I-NA-JA-PA-QA

This phrase is occasionally added after the word sire. It appears to be a designation of the city in which the king resided (in Japaqa). The Latin root PAG can mean province, district, or village.

Complete Phrase

jus-tice / law / order	**sar** / mun duty	un-arch / **mon-arch** / king	natal	eponym	sire	in	pag
JA-SA	SA-RA-ME	U-NA-RU-KA	NA-TI	I-PI-NA-MA	SI-RU-TE	I-NA	JA-PA-QA
by **order**	of **duty** to	**monarch**	**born**	**upon the name**	**sire**	**in**	**Japaqa**

26

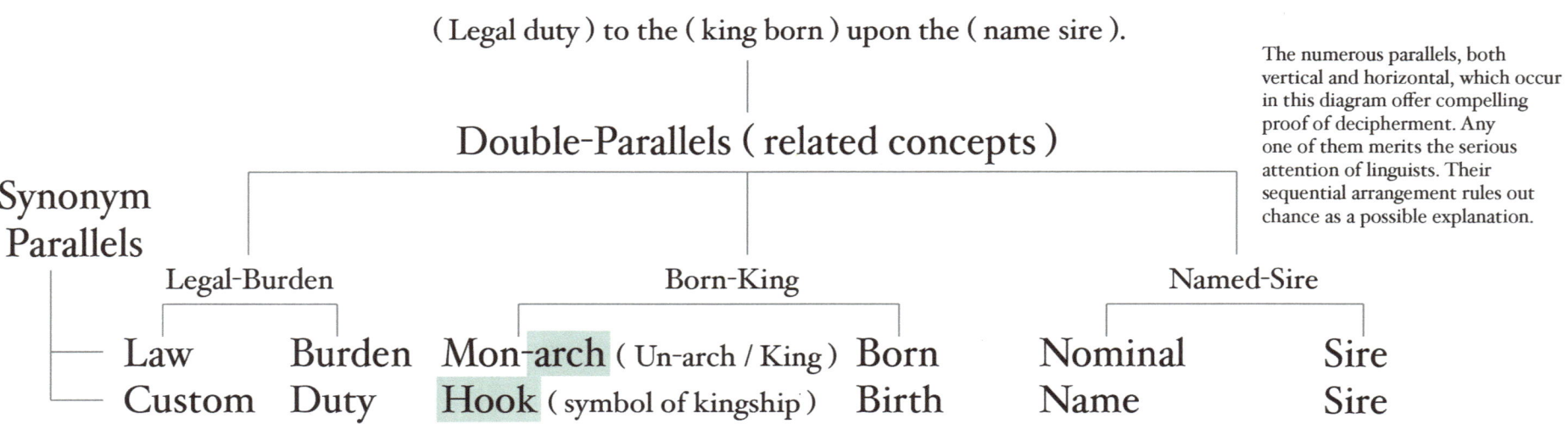

Triple-Parallel (coherent phrase / the king's authority)

(Legal duty) to the (king born) upon the (name sire).

Double-Parallels (related concepts)

Synonym Parallels

	Legal-Burden		Born-King		Named-Sire	
	Law	Burden	Mon-arch (Un-arch / King)	Born	Nominal	Sire
	Custom	Duty	Hook (symbol of kingship)	Birth	Name	Sire

The numerous parallels, both vertical and horizontal, which occur in this diagram offer compelling proof of decipherment. Any one of them merits the serious attention of linguists. Their sequential arrangement rules out chance as a possible explanation.

Sequential Consonant-Parallels

	1	2	3	4	5	6
j = i consonant	I()S	S()R	()N-()RC	N()T	()P()-N()M()N	S()R
	()S	S()R	()NC	N()S	()P()-N()M	S()R
	()S	M()N				
	ius / us	sar / mun	un-arc / unc	nat / nas	eponym / name-nomen	seior (sire)

= Uniquely occurring synonym pairs extrapolated from the consonants shown above.

The first three consonant-parallels shown here each yield a single possible synonym pair in Latin. The fourth consonant-parallel produces two: nit/nis and nat/nas. The former can be ruled out because the inscriptions say NA, and there is no reason to suspect a vowel change. The vowel changes observed in some of the other words will be discussed in the next chapter. The fifth parallel is remarkable in that when the search is expanded to English a double singularity occurs. First, the only word matching the given consonants is **eponym** (upon the name). And second, the only pair matching N-M / N-M-N is **name / nomen** (both meaning name). The sixth parallel is simply the same word occurring twice. Both its context and original vowel (I) suggest that the word is **sire**.

2. Alphabetic Conversion

Alphabetic Conversion

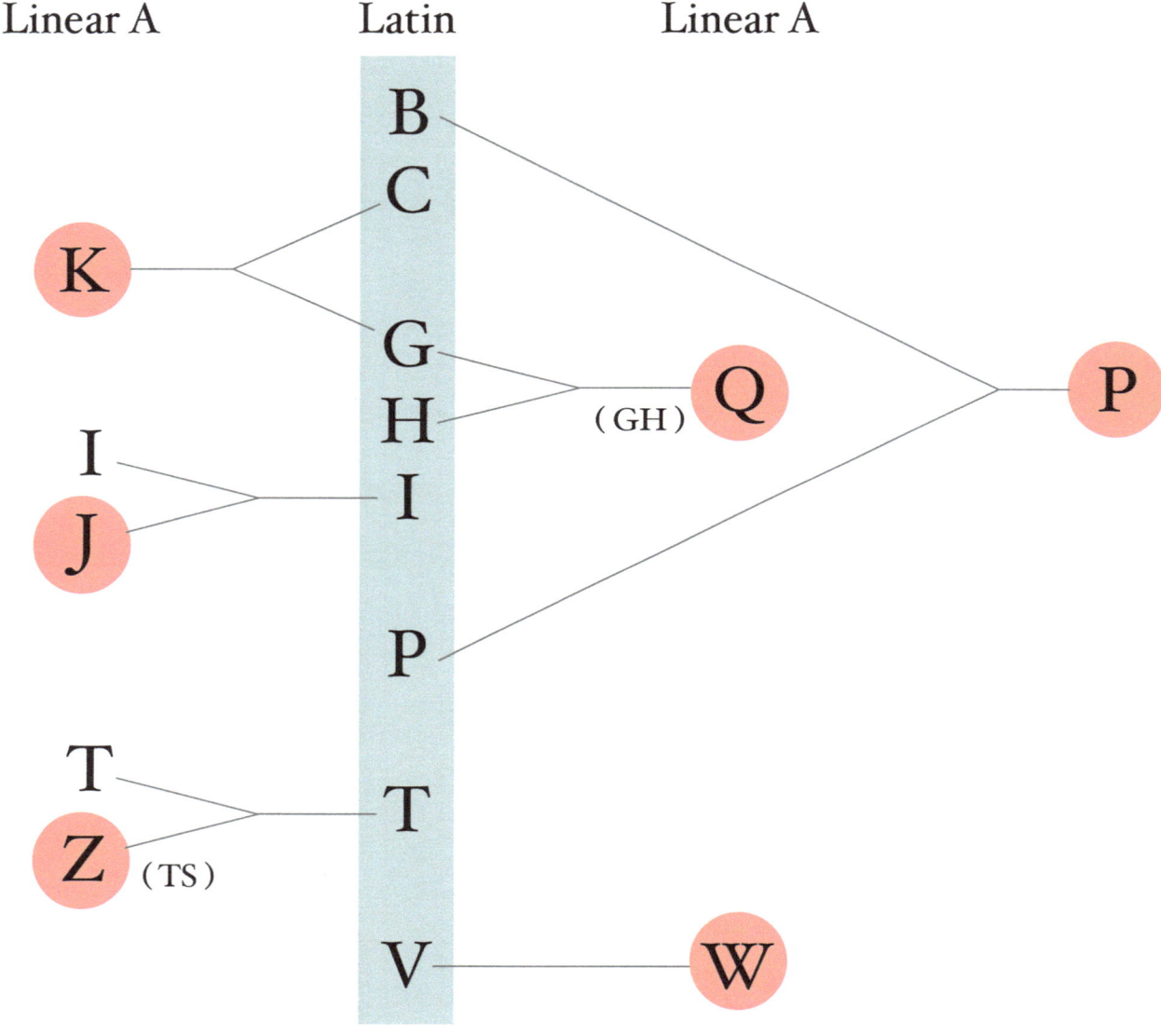

The consonant changes in this diagram are required simply because of letters which are not shared between the two writing systems.

K = C and G

	Example	Example
Latin	CANTATE	DICITE
Linear A	A-KA-NU-ZA-TI	A-DI-KI-TE-TE

Z becomes T in Latin

C

K

G

	Example	Example
Latin	GUTTA	AGITATE
Linear A	KU-ZU	JA-NA-KI-TE-TE

Z becomes T in Latin   Prefix

C and G were not differentiated in writing[7] until a thousand years after the Linear A script was in use. Early Latin continued the practice of writing these closely related sounds as a single sign. Eventually a stroke was added to the letter C to form G, distinguishing them more precisely. The letter C is represented phonetically by K in Linear A. Thus K in Linear A = C and G in Latin.

Unknown Syllable *301 = NG

(as hinted at by the T / N letter coupling shared among first stage words in the ritual sequence)

T / N partial coupling

Prefix	Stage 1	Stage 2
A-	TA-I-*301	WA-JA
JA-	TA-I-*301	WA-JA
A-NA-	T I - *301	WA-JA
(A)-NA-	T U - *301	NE
	TA-NA-I-*301	U-TI-NU
	TA-NA-I-*301	TI
	TA-NA	SU-TE
	TA-NU	MU-TI
	(TA)NU	PA-E

	I-(*301)	WA-JA

T / N complete coupling if *301 = NG sound

Prefix	Stage 1	Stage 2
A-	TA-I-*301	WA-JA
JA-	TA-I-*301	WA-JA
A-NA-	T I - *301	WA-JA
(A)-NA-	T U - *301	NE
	TA-NA-I-*301	U-TI-NU
	TA-NA-I-*301	TI
	TA-NA	SU-TE
	TA-NU	MU-TI
	(TA)NU	PA-E

	I-(*301)	WA-JA

Syllable *301 = NG (Results)

The relationships that occur within and between ritual sequence stages as a result of the NG substitution.

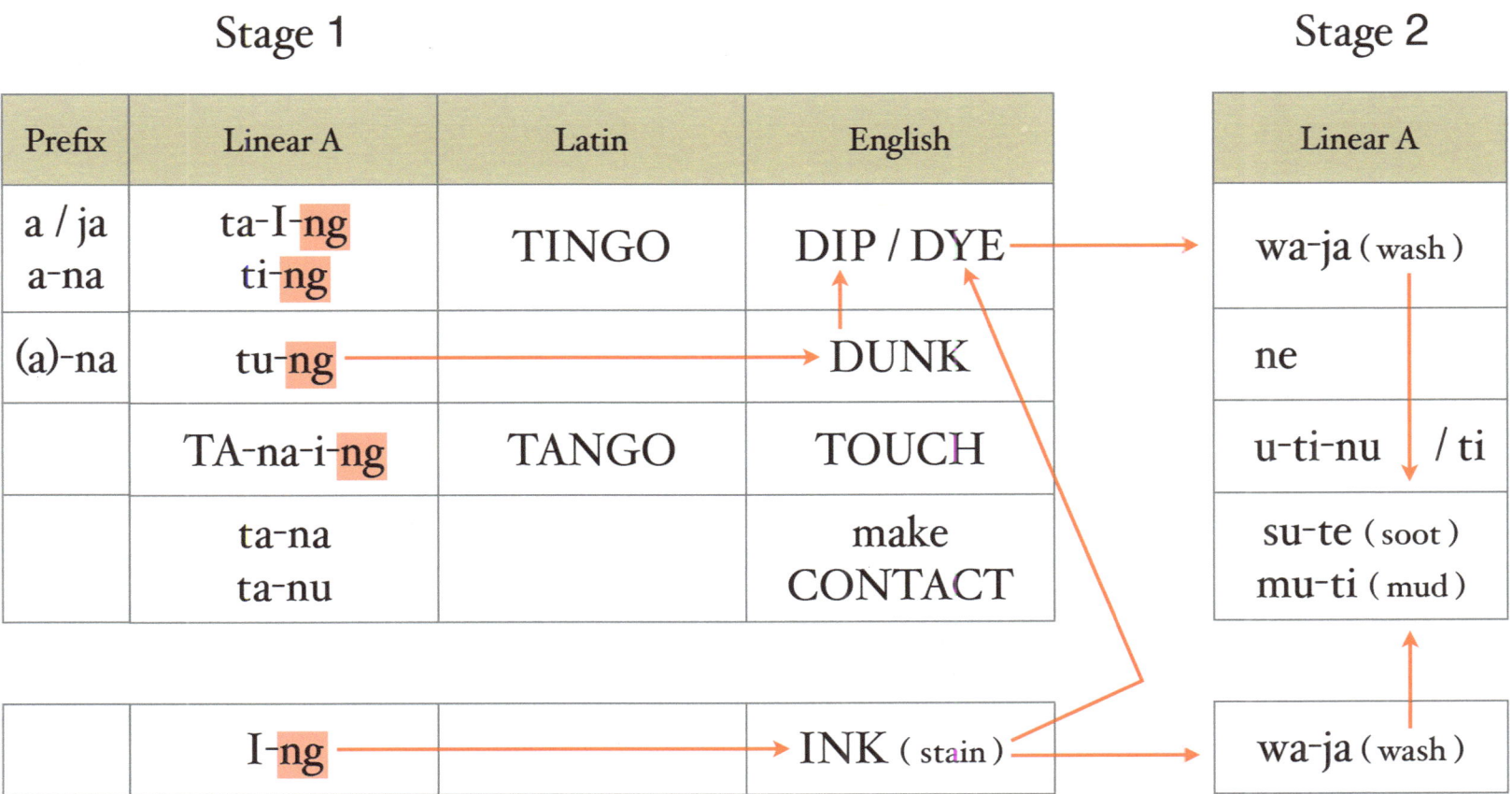

The NG syllable most likely ends with a vowel. There are several examples of double consonant to single vowel groupings in Linear A, and no syllable in the script lacks a vowel entirely. The identity of the unknown vowel is of little significance because it occurs after the root.

Diphthongs and Dual-Syllables

1. Diphthong conventions in Linear A appear to differ from those found in Linear B.

2. Some signs in Linear A function as dual-syllables. They assume the role of other signs which are missing from the syllabary. During the transition to Linear B, several of these dual-syllables were decoupled by the addition of new signs. Some confusion over syllable assignments, particularly O / U and their related diphthongs, may be a result of that separation.

Diphthongs	ai	ei	oi	au	eu	ou
Linear A Orthography	I	I	U	AU	U	U
Linear B Orthography [8]	A	E	O	AU	EU	OU

In Linear A, the second vowel of a diphthong is indicated rather than the first. This practice may extend beyond the vowel pairs in this diagram.

Un-Arc /
oU-NA-RU-KA = mon-arch
(oi)

MaI-DA = maid

MaI-RI-NA-RA = mariner

Due to repeated orthographic confusion of O and U, it is difficult to be sure of the intended pronunciation of UN-ARC. A parallel with the word UNC makes its meaning certain regardless of pronunciation.

eI-JA = (demonstrative)
(JO)
                               *eja/ejo [9]

WeI-PI = *weip [5] (Proto-Indo-European) / VIB - vibrare (Latin)

The signs NO, JO, DO, and MO do not exist in the Linear A syllabary. Their sounds are assigned to NA, JA, DU, and MU. The latter retain their original values and thus function as dual-syllables. This resolves their conflicts with O pronunciations in Proto-Italic and Proto-Indo-European reconstructions. It also explains the conspicuous absence of O syllables in Linear A. With the arrival of Linear B, all O syllables were given dedicated signs.

eI-PI-NA-MA = eponym (epi + onoma in Greek)   *nomn [6]
(NO)

SeI-RU = sire / seior (Latin)

JA-SA = iussu (by order in Latin)   *jowos [10]
(JO)

A-SA = usu (by custom in Latin)

} → The words A-SA and JA-SA are used in parallel and may have been formed by affixing A / JA to a common root. In the word A-SA, the choice of the vowel A rather than the expected O (which was available in this case) was perhaps due to an orthographic association with JA = JO in the word JA-SA.

DU-MI-NE = domina (lady in Latin)   *dom/dem [5]
(DO)

MU-NE = munus (duty in Latin)   *moinos [5]
(MO)

Some vowel conflicts could be attributable to orthographic depth or to the uncertainty inherent in linguistic models.

3. Affixes

Prefix / Suffix	Definition	Examples
A	to / into / toward	KN Zc 7 KO Za 1 PK Za 11 TL Za 1
JA	cause to be / make it so / to make	IO Za 2 KE Zb 4 PK Za 8 PK Za 16 ZA Zb 34
I-JA (demonstrative)	to be / to be for	CR Zf 1 IO Za 5 KN Za 10 PR Za 1
I	for	IO Za 2 KN Zf 31 KO Za 1 PK Za 8
DA	from the / (gift)	KN Zf 31
DE	of	KO Zf 2
DI	from	KN Zf 13
DU (noun-forming prefix)	Indo-European / English - do (causation of process)	KN Za 10 KN Zc 7 PK Za 11

Prefix / Suffix	Definition	Examples
ME (genitive / possessive)	of / of + to	IO Za 6 PK Za 11 TL Za 1 ZA Zg 35
TA SI / SE	the	IO Za 2 KN Zf 31 ARKH Zf 9 / CR Zf 1
TE	a / the	PK Za 11
TI	is + to	KN Zf 31
TO	the	KO Zf 2
QA (kʷha)	who is	KN Zf 31
TA-I-ZU	this	IO Za 6
TE-SU	these	KN Zf 31
I-NA	in	IO Za 6
AU-TA	out	KO Zf 2
AU	away	ZA Zg 35

All of these affixes have left traces in European languages.

Affixes and Word Order

Affixes are an essential element of the Linear A script and affect word order when translating into English.

Prefixed Verbs
(the verb takes priority)

For Prefixed Verbs: Word Order (in English) = Verb, Prefix, Noun

unless the verb is followed by an article, which links it to the noun before the prefix

PK Za 11				PK Za 8			
	2	1	3		2	1	3
	Prefix	Verb	Noun	The prefix can be a verb, such as JA, even after another verb.	Prefix	Verb	Noun
The prefix can be a preposition such as A.	to / into	dip	water		to make	stir	purification

IO Za 2				PK Za 11			
	2	1	3	4	1	2	3
	Prefix	Verb	Noun	Prefix	Verb	Article	Noun
The prefix can be an article such as TA.	the	convey	ringing noise (perhaps caused by stirring)	to	speak	a	blessing

Affixes can also be attached to nouns and adjectives in Linear A. Their behavior appears to be dependent on the structure of the sentence and the meaning of each particular affix being used. These are discussed in more detail as annotations in the translated texts themselves.

Prefixes and the Consecutive Vowel Rule

Some prefixes add a final consonant if the next word begins with a vowel:

JA-NA-KI-TE-TE / I-ZU-RI-NI-TA / I-DA-PA-I-SA-RI

	Linear A Prefix / Word 1	Vowel to Vowel Interruption Consonant	Linear A Word 2	Latin / English	Meaning
PK Za 8	JA	N	A-KI-TE-TE	agitate	stir

PH 6	I-NA-WA				in water
	A-RI				
	I	Z	U-RI-NI-TA	urino	to plunge / to wet
	A-RI				
	I	D	A-PA-I-SA-RI	appeaser(s)	priest(s) / priestess(es)

Z may be part of the root in this example, although it is later dropped in Latin.

English: (an agitation)	a	→ agitation	incorrect
	an	→ agitation	correct
Italian: (and agitated)	e	→ agitato	incorrect
	ed	→ agitato	correct

4. The Ritual Sequence
Synonym Analysis

Speaking Synonyms

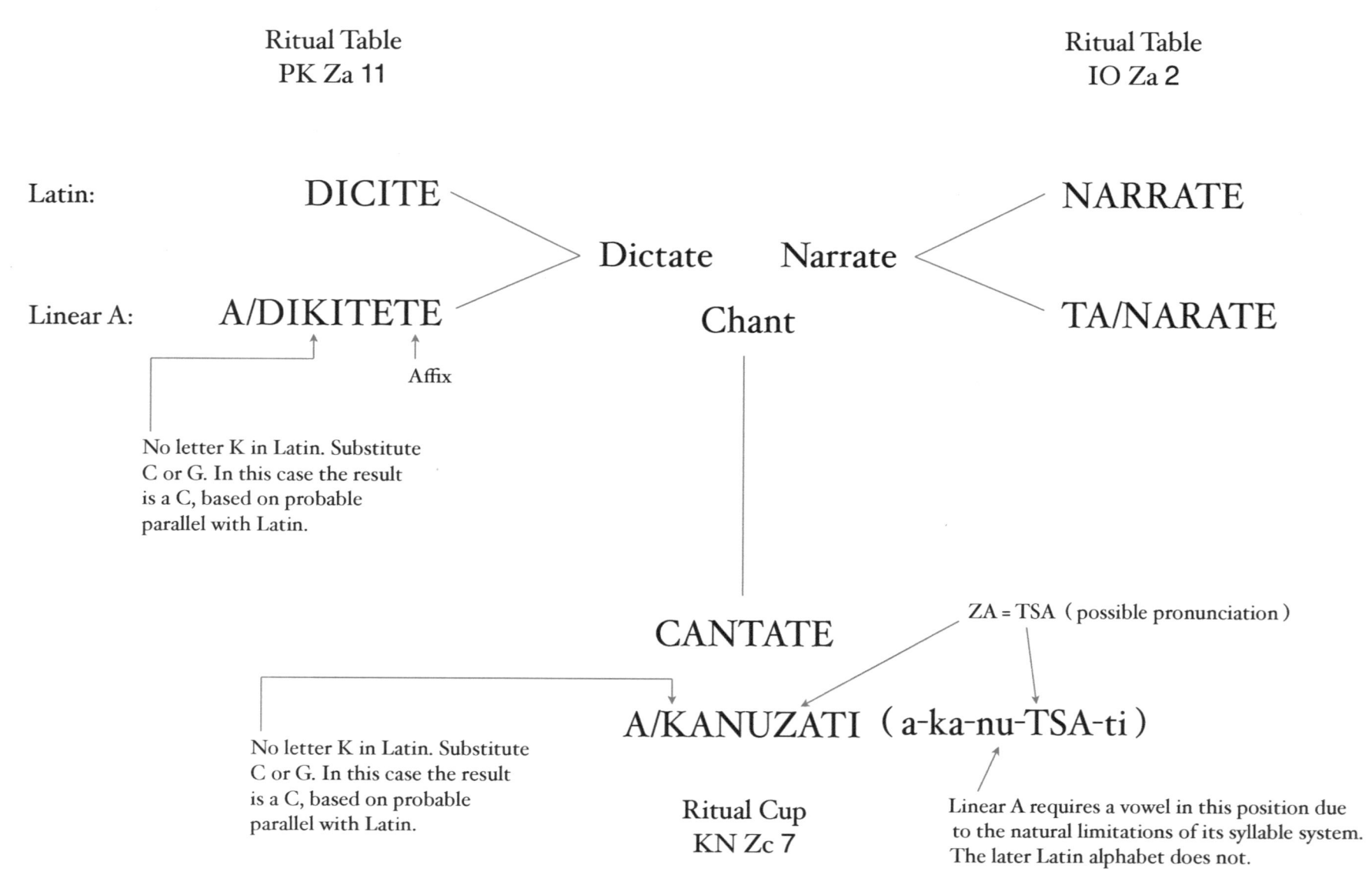

Stirring Synonyms

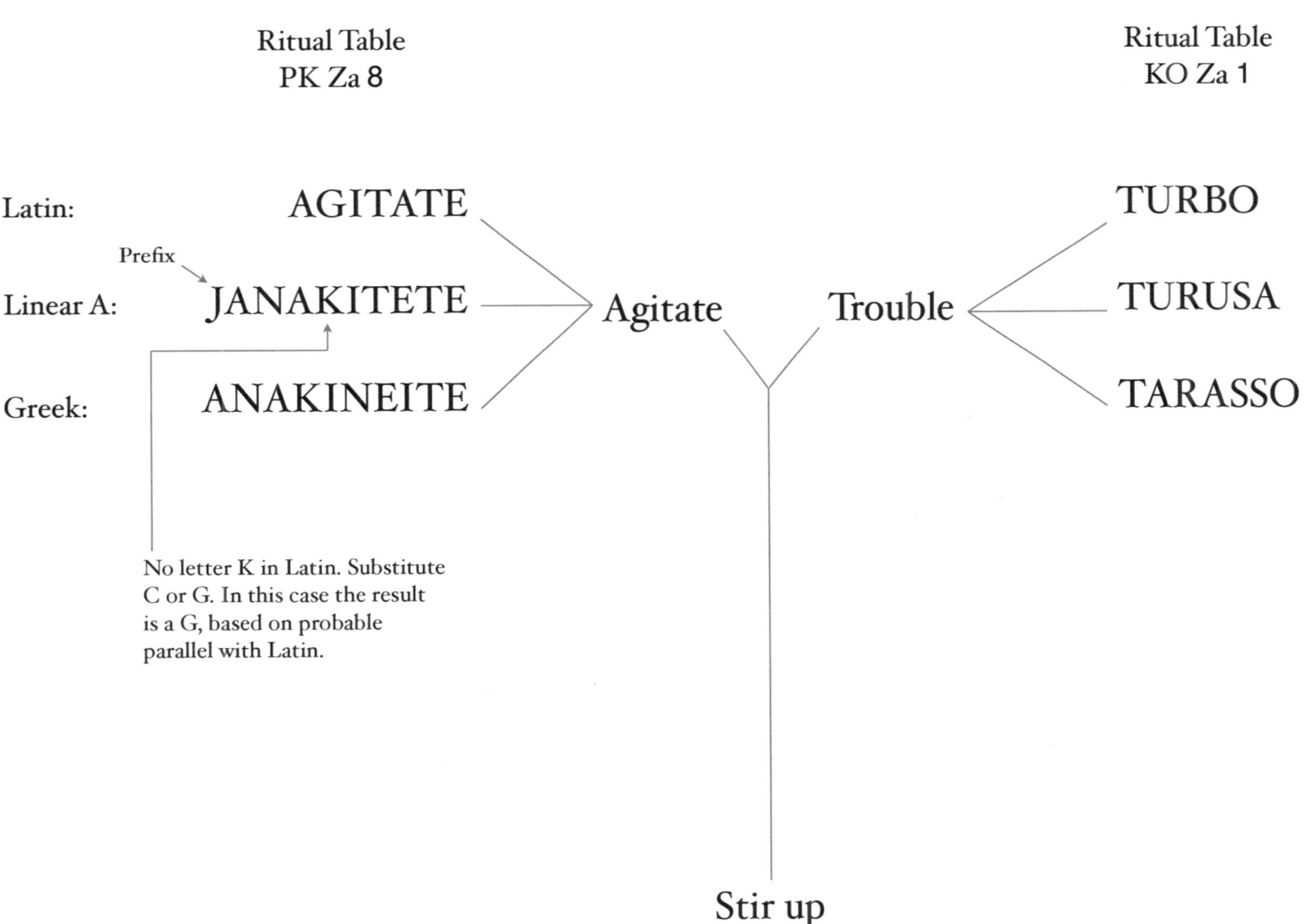

Stirring Synonyms

Ritual Table PK Za 8   Ritual Table KO Za 1

Latin: AGITATE   TURBO

Prefix →

Linear A: JANAKITETE → Agitate   Trouble ← TURUSA

Greek: ANAKINEITE   TARASSO

The dictionary entry on the right illustrates the close relationship of the words **agitate** and **trouble**. It also links them directly with the ancient Greek word **tarasso** through the idea of **stirring water**. The diagram above shows a pair of ritual tables with two Linear A words closely resembling Greek and Latin words for stirring. The odds of this happening by chance seem low.

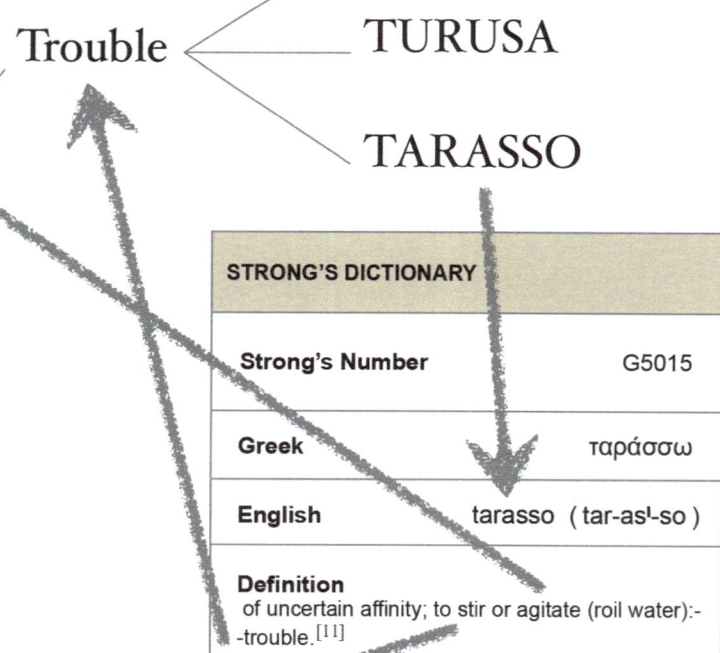

STRONG'S DICTIONARY	
Strong's Number	G5015
Greek	ταράσσω
English	tarasso (tar-as'-so)
Definition	of uncertain affinity; to stir or agitate (roil water):- -trouble.[11]

Stir up

A-TA-I-NG / TA-NA-I-NG / TA-NU

The relationship among first stage words, in the ritual sequence, which contain the letters T and N.

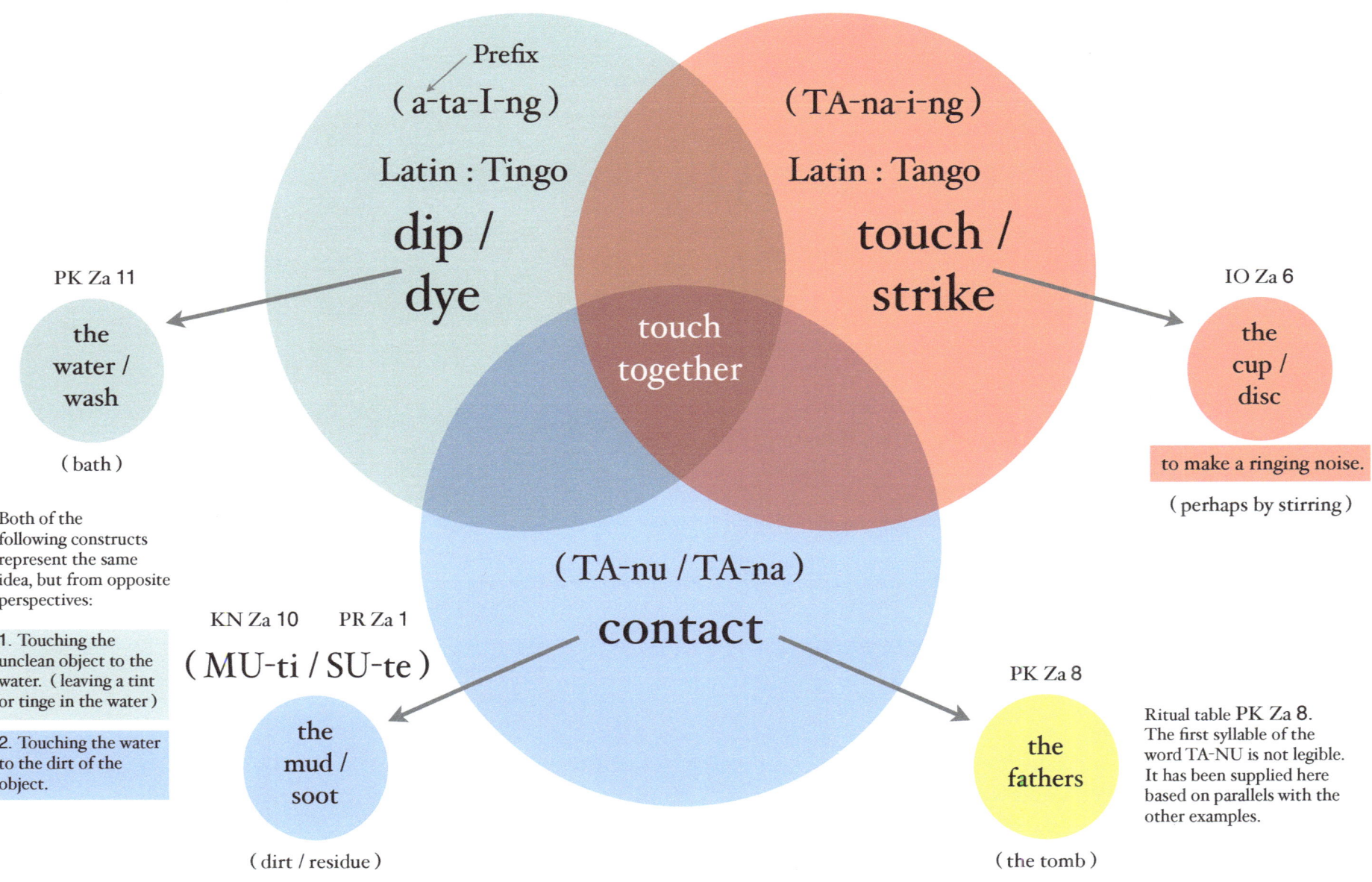

A-TA-I-NG / WA-JA

First stage word divisions in the ritual sequence.

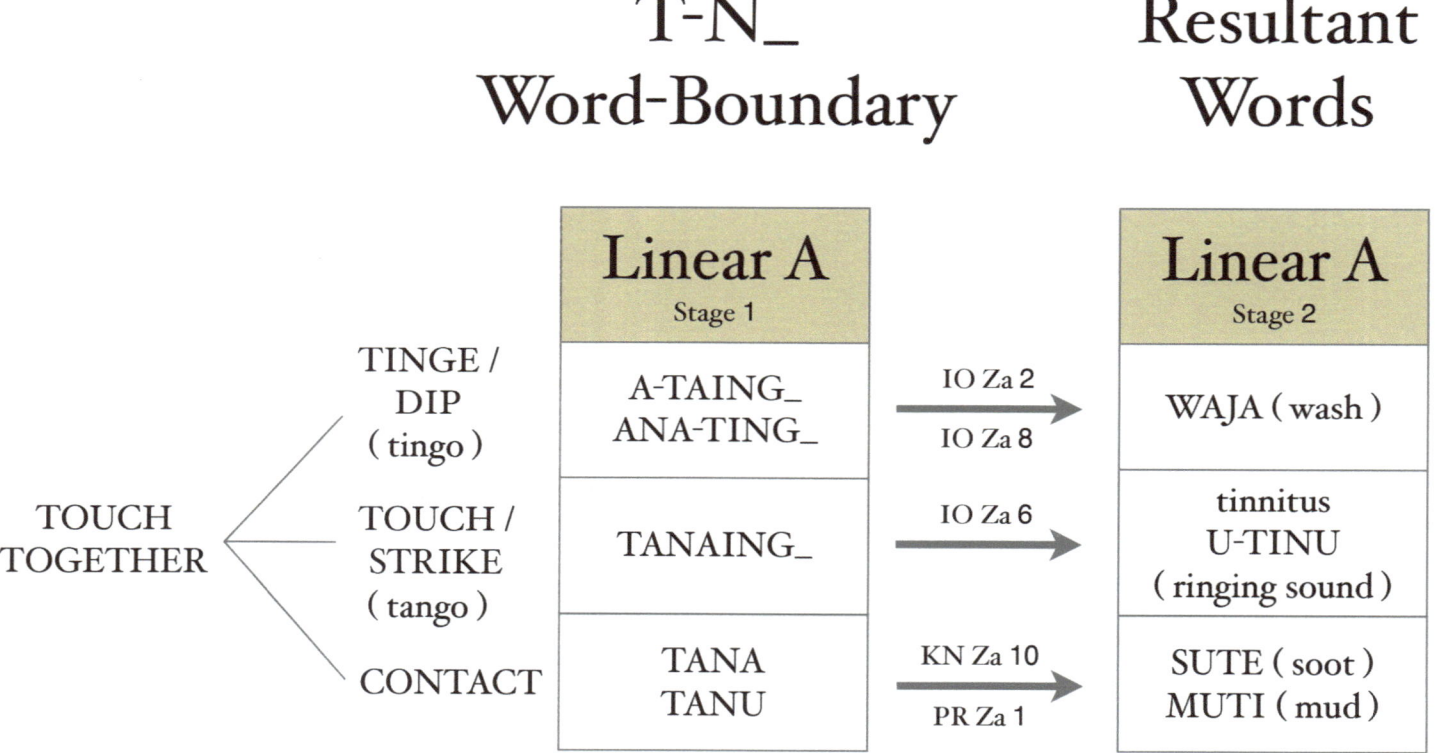

The next few pages progress through successive stages of the ritual sequence. The ritual sequence includes and expands on the series of parallels previously described. Its complete form will be shown on a chart after all of the stages have been presented.

DU-PU-RE / DU-RA-RE
Root Isolation

Shared Letters

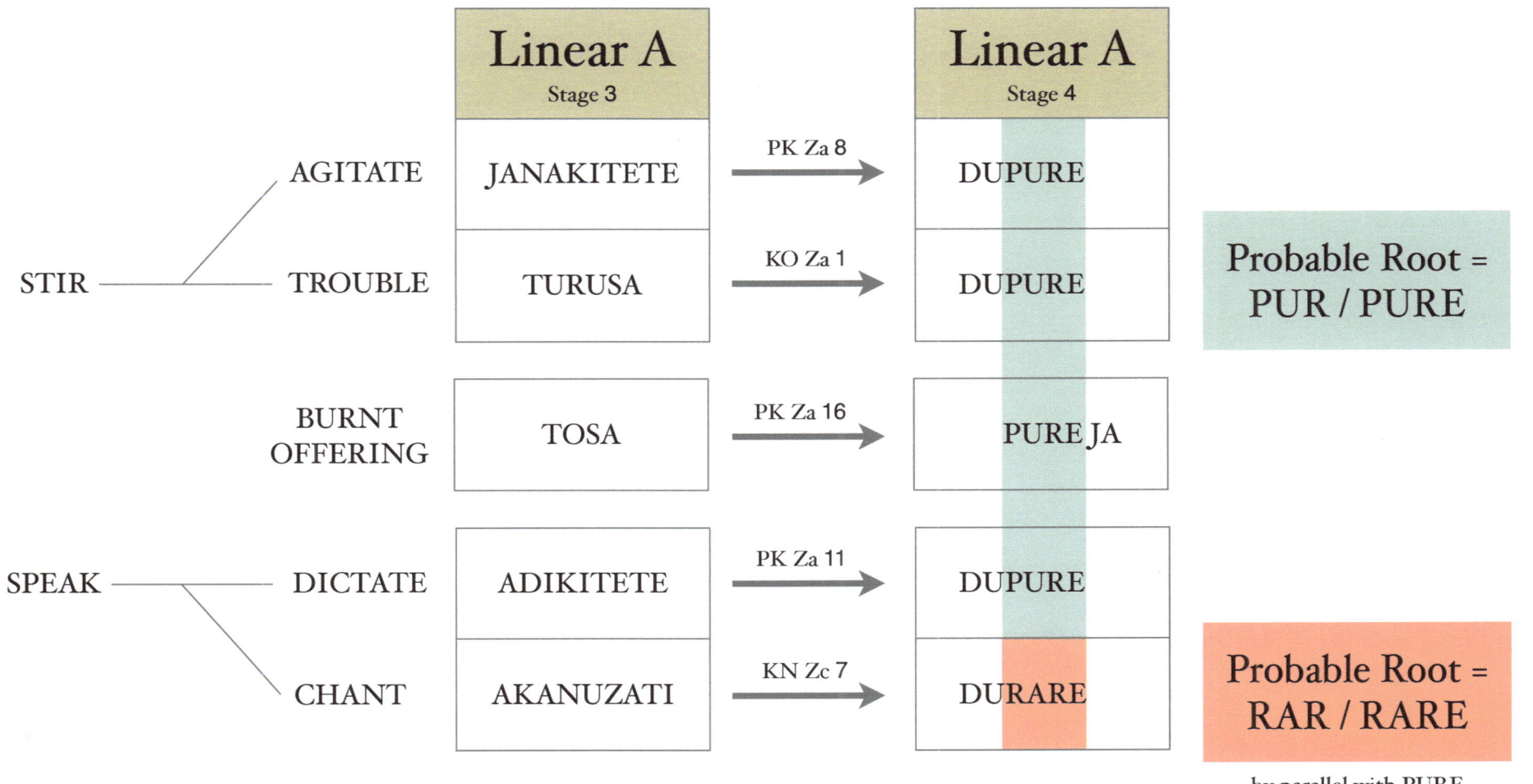

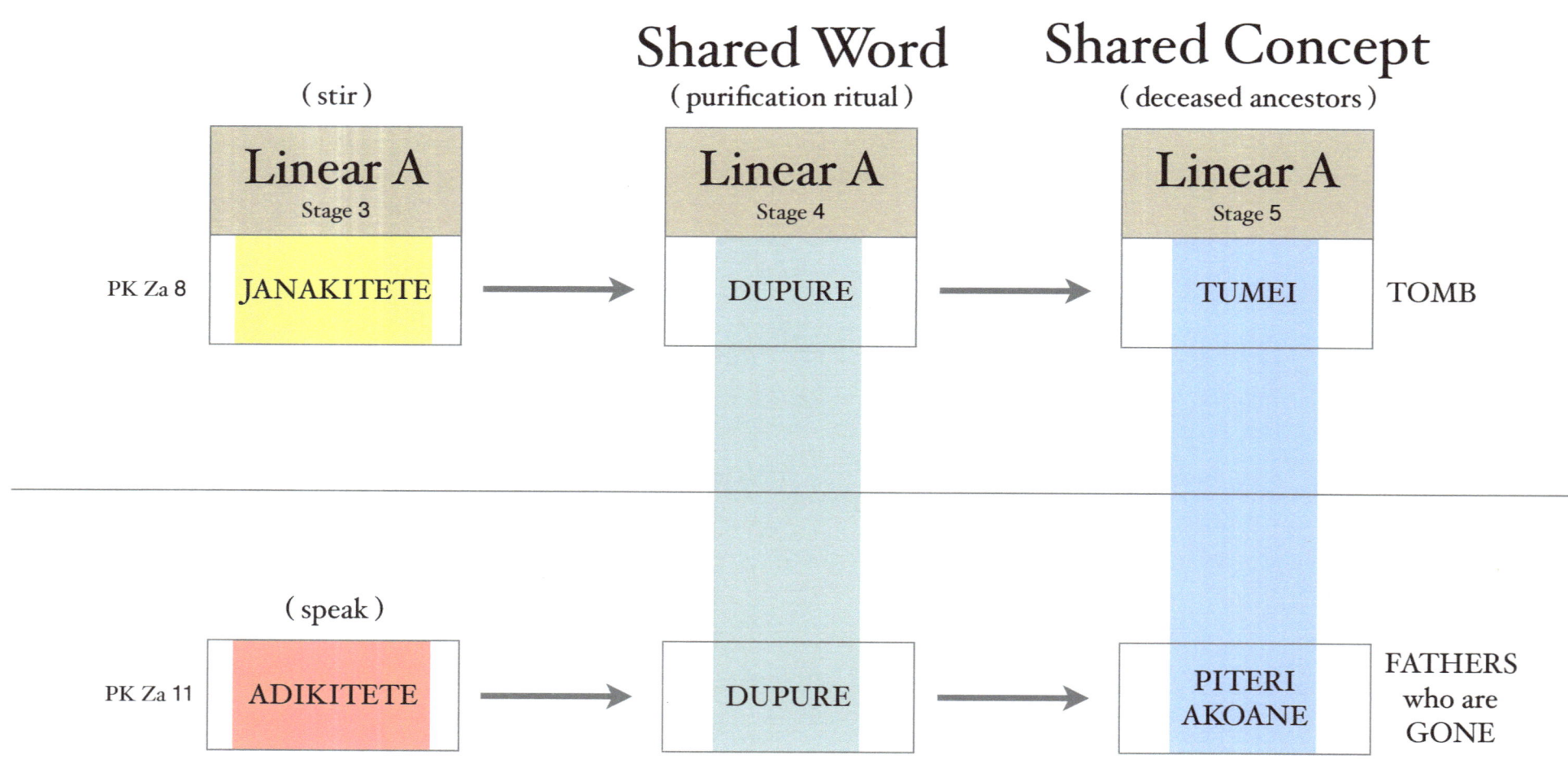

JA-SA / A-SA
SA-RA / MU-NE

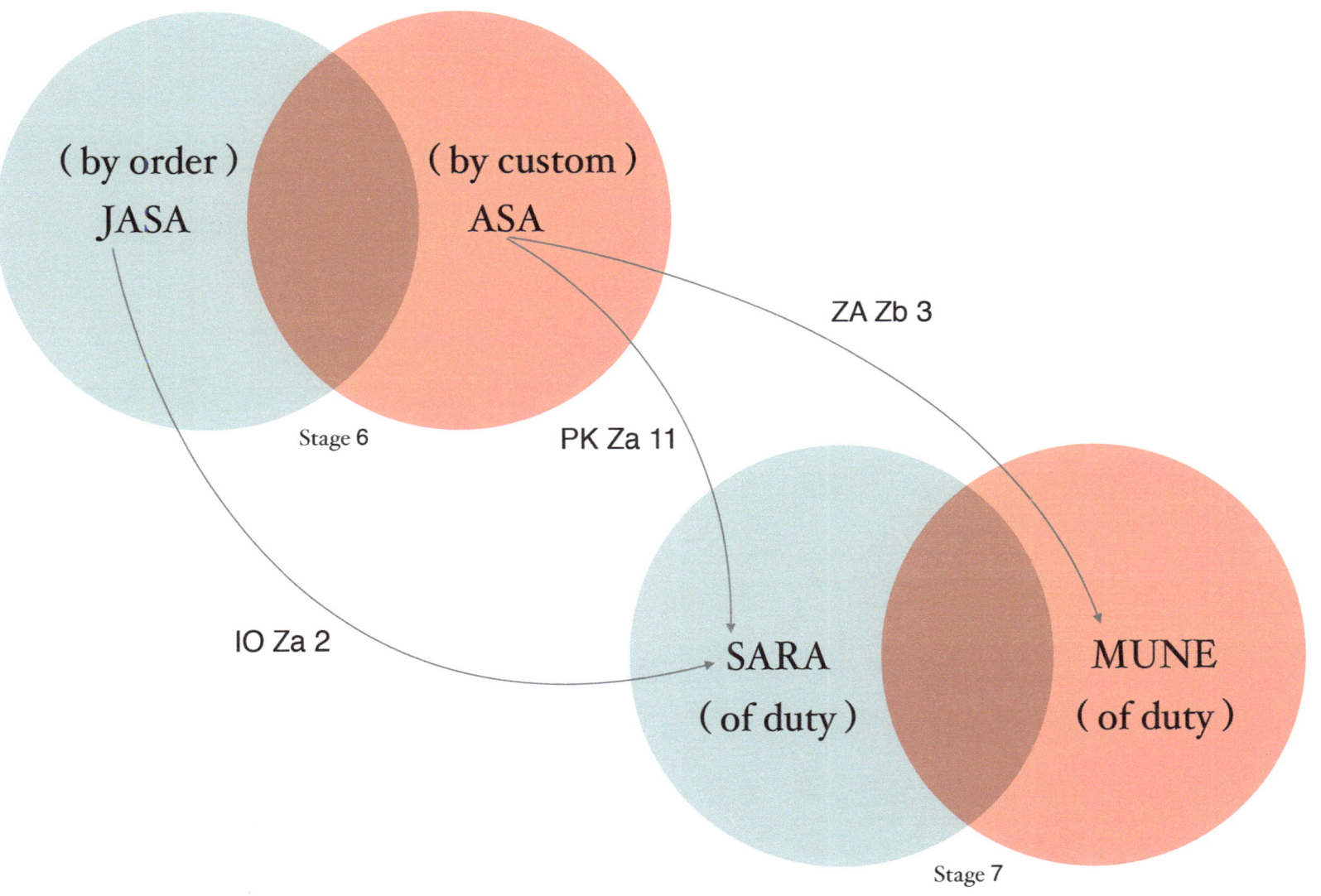

The Ritual Sequence

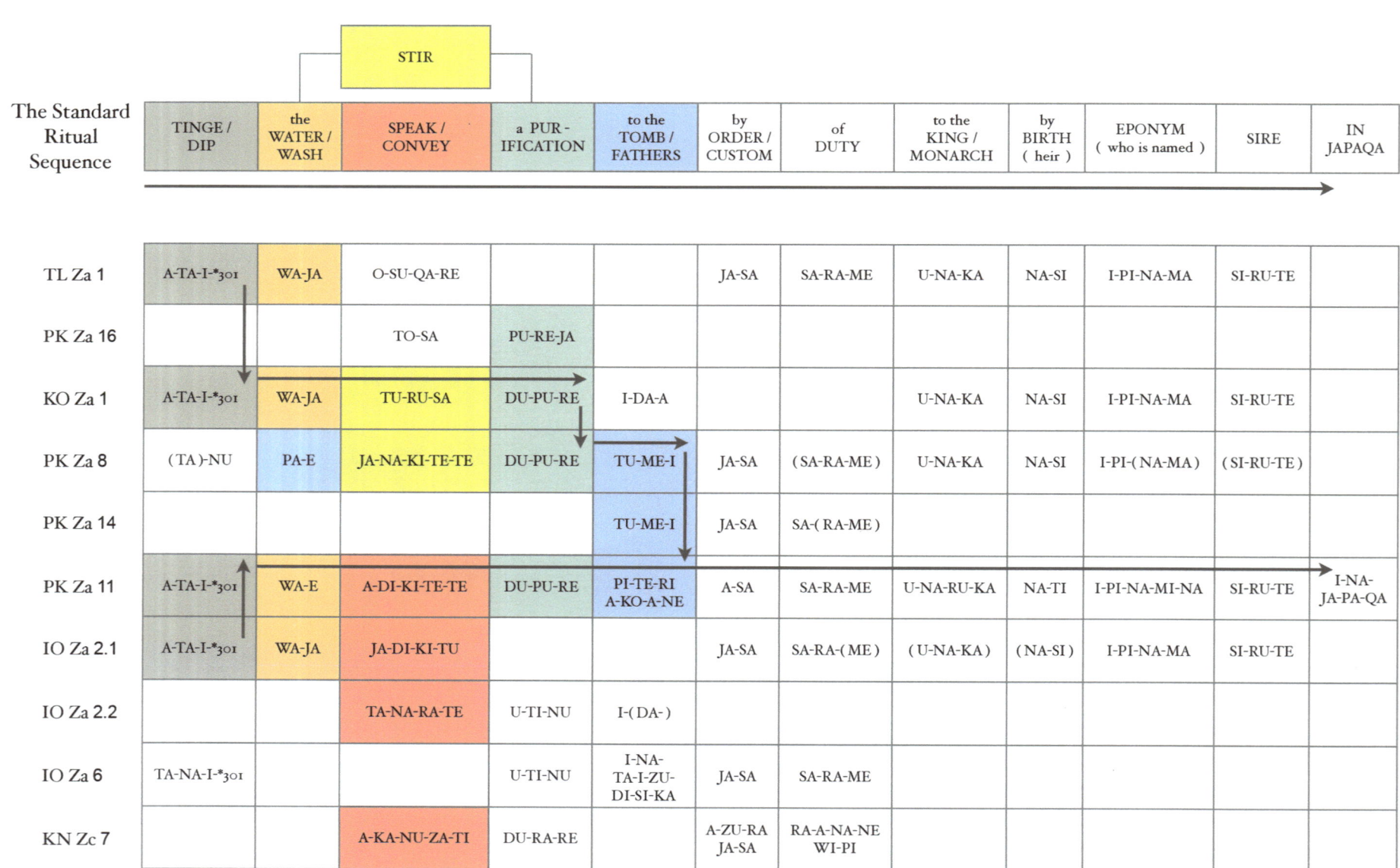

5. Vocabulary

Linear A	Latin : English	Linear A	Latin : English
A-TA-I-*301 (a-ta-I-ng) TA-NA-I-*301 (TA-na-i-ng)	tingo : to tinge (dip / dye) tango : to touch	NA-TI NA-SI	natio : birth nasci : to be born
WA-E WA-JA	aqua : water —— : wash	I-PI-NA-MA (Greek epi + onoma) I-PI-NA-MI-NA (Latin nomen)	—— : eponym —— : eponym
A-DI-KI-TE-TE TA-NA-RA-TE A-KA-NU-ZA-TI (a-ka-nu-TSA-ti)	dicite : to say or speak narrate : to tell or relate cantate : to chant or sing	SI-RU-TE	seior : sire
		I-NA JA-PA-QA	in : in Japaqa (city name)
PU-RE-JA DU-PU-RE	purus : pure —— : purification	(Greek) JA-NA-KI-TE-TE (ANAKINEITE) TU-RU-SA (TARASSO)	agitate : to agitate, trouble, or stir turbo : to trouble
PI-TE-RI / PA-E PA-JA-TA-RI / PA-JA	pater : father(s) —— : forefather(s) or leader(s)		
TU-ME-I / TU-ME A-KO-A-NE	tumba : tomb —— : gone (i.e. fathers who are gone, deceased)	U-TI-NU	tinnitus : tinkle, jingle, ringing noise (perhaps caused by stirring in a cup)
A-SA JA-SA (j = i)	usu : use, usual (by custom) iussu : justice, law (by order)	O-SU-QA-RE I-ZU-RI-NI-TA	sugere : to soak up urino : to plunge into water
SA-RA MU-NE	sarcina : burden (i.e. duty, obligation) Proto-Indo-European base **sai** : suffering munus : duty, obligation	A-DI-DA-KI-TI TI-DI-TE-QA-TI DI-DI-KA-SE	—— : dedicate —— : dedicated —— : dedication
U-NA-RU-KA U-NA-KA	un + arcus : king or monarch (one + arch) uncus : hook (Linear B wanaka : king)	English : one + arch (i.e. sole leader : monarch) from Greek Linear A : un + aruka (Linear A requires a vowel between R and K) Latin : unus + arcus (roots isolated theoretically = un-ark like Linear A) Greek : monos + arkhos (roots isolated = mon-arch)	

Germanic	Linear A	English
ja	JA	(yes) cause to be
tunken	TU-(NG_)-NE	dunk
*strauma [5]	SE-TE-RI-MU	stream
*saiwiz [6]	TA/ SA-ZA	seas
wasser	WA-SA WA-SI	water
wasche	WA-JA	wash
*mud [6]	MU-TI	mud
*sotan [6]	SU-TE (SO)	soot
maid	MI-DA	maid
*in [5]	I-NA	in
*ut [5]	AU-TA	out
dies	TA-I-ZU	this
diese	TE-SU	these
gehen	A-KO-A-NE	go / ago gone

Minoan vocabulary is characteristically Italic, with a substantial Germanic component. The Basque words shown below are not intended to suggest a direct relationship with Minoan language. However, in view of their appropriateness to the sentences in which they occur, some of them may be loan-words.

Basque [12]	Linear A	English
irentsi	A-RE-NE-SI	rinse swallow
itsaso	TA/SA-ZA	seas
ama	A-MA	ma / mother
aitaren	PA-JA-TA-RI (PA-IA-TA-RI)	fathers forefathers
abiega	PI-KE (BI-GE)	mighty big (great)
zauria	ZA-RE	sore / wound
apaiz	A-PA-I-SA-RI	appeaser(s) priest / priestess

Related Parallel Vocabulary

Possible origin of the word **king**.

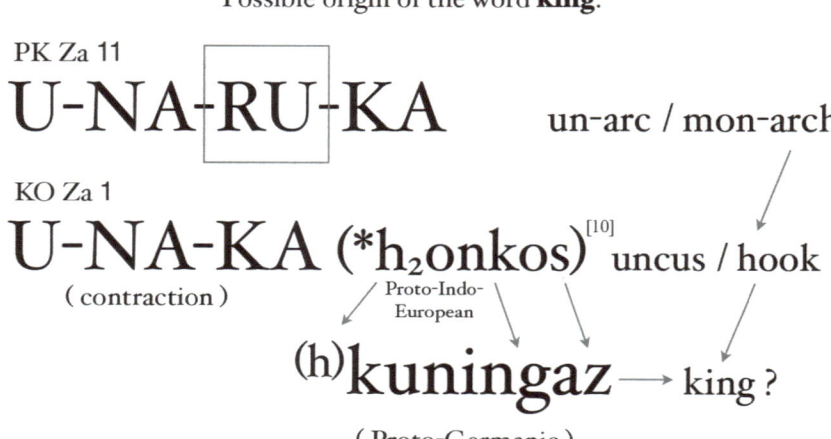

PK Za 11
U-NA-RU-KA   un-arc / mon-arch

KO Za 1
U-NA-KA (*h₂onkos)[10] uncus / hook
(contraction)

Proto-Indo-European

(h)kuningaz → king?
(Proto-Germanic)

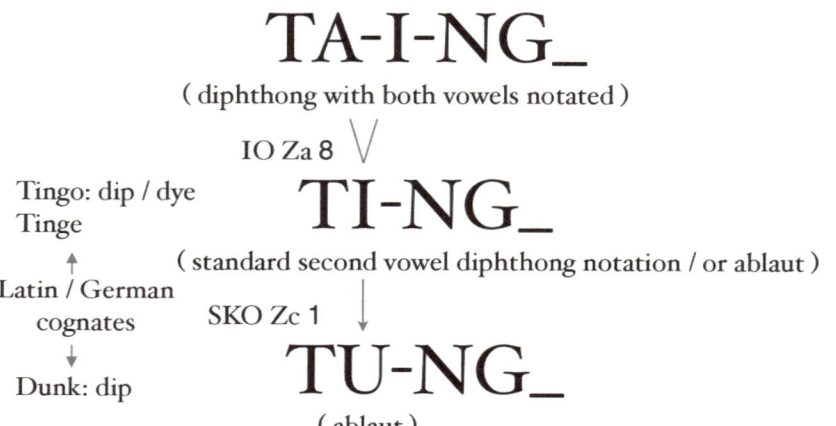

PK Za 11
TA-I-NG_
(diphthong with both vowels notated)

IO Za 8
TI-NG_
(standard second vowel diphthong notation / or ablaut)

Tingo: dip / dye
Tinge

Latin / German cognates

Dunk: dip

SKO Zc 1
TU-NG_
(ablaut)

PK Za 12. The text is not entirely clear on this artifact. It may contain either a space or an extra syllable. (NA) is suggested by John Younger.[1] The scenario shown here lends support to that reading.

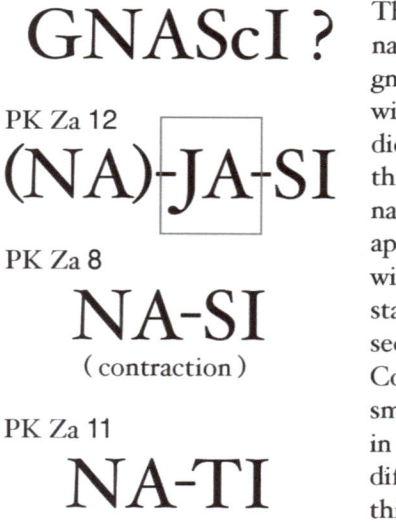

GNAScI ?

PK Za 12
(NA)-JA-SI

PK Za 8
NA-SI
(contraction)

PK Za 11
NA-TI

The word-forms nas, nat, and gnas / gnat are listed within a single dictionary entry for the Latin word nascor.[4] They also appear in Linear A within the same stage of the ritual sequence. Considering the small corpus of text in Linear A, it is difficult to ascribe this to chance.

A sense of context is necessary in order to translate the Minoan words DU-PU-RE and DU-RA-RE. They are likely formed from the Proto-Indo-European roots *dhe,[6] *peu,[6] and *rar.[5] DU-PU-RE occurs in the context of ritual washing. The word DU-RA-RE is linked with chanting or singing. Both words are found in sentences where the surrounding text implies that they are nouns, yet they resemble adjectives. The dual-syllable DU / DO (English **do**) relates to causation of process and may be converting the adjectives into the required nouns.

The context is washing.
                                    pure (clean)
                                    + do (causation)
  PK Za 8   DU-PU-RE: = (purification)

The context is musical.
                                   rare (having intervals between)[5]
                                    + do (causation)
  KN Zc 7   DU-RA-RE: = (rhythm)

6. Artifact Translations

Ritual Tables
PK Za 11, IO Za 2, PK Za 8, and KO Za 1

PK Za 11
Heraklion Archeological Museum – HM 1341

PK Za 11

A-TA-I-*301-WA-E A-DI-KI-TE-TE-DU-PU-RE PI-TE-RI A-KO-A-NE

A-SA-SA-RA-ME U-NA-RU-KA-NA-TI I-PI-NA-MI-NA SI-RU-TE I-NA-JA-PA-QA

Translation Process

Linear A : A-TA-I-*301- / WA-E / A-DI-KI-TE / TE / DU-PU-RE / PI-TE-RI / A-KO-A-NE /
(with NG_ notation above A-DI-KI-TE)

Literal Text : (dip - to) (water) (dictate - a - purification - to) (fathers) (ago / gone)

Translation : (dip into) (water) : (speak a blessing to) (fathers) (who are gone) :

A-SA / SA-RA-ME / U-NA-RU-KA / NA-TI / I-PI-NA-MI-NA / SI-RU-TE / I-NA / JA-PA-QA

(by custom) (of duty - to) (monarch) (by birth) (eponym) (sire) (in) (Japaqa)

(by custom) (of duty to) (the king) (heir) (who is named) (sire) (in) (Japaqa)

Final Translation

Dip into the water.

Speak a blessing to our fathers who are gone, by custom of duty to the king heir who is named sire in Japaqa.

IO Za 2

A-TA-I-*301-WA-JA JA-DI-KI-TU JA-SA-SA-RA-(?) (?) I-PI-NA-MA SI-RU-TE TA-NA-RA-TE-U-TI-NU I-(?)

Translation Process

Linear A: A-TA-I-*301-^(NG_) / WA-JA / JA-DI-KI-TU / JA-SA / SA-RA-me / u-na-ka /

Literal Text: (dip-to) (wash) (make-dictate) (by order) (of duty-to) (king)

Translation: (dip into) (wash) : (make declaration) (by order) (of duty to) (the king)

na-si / I-PI-NA-MA / SI-RU-TE / TA-NA-RA-TE / U-TI-NU ——→ IO Za 11 U-TI-NU / I-NA / I-DA-( ) → I-da-( )

(born) (eponym) (sire) (narrate / make known - the) (ringing noise) (for - gift / offering)

(heir) (who is named) (sire) : (convey a) (ringing noise) (for the offering)

Final Translation

Dip into the wash.

Make a declaration, by order of duty to the king heir who is named sire. Convey a ringing noise for the offering.

PK Za 8

(?)-NU PA-E JA-NA-KI-TE-TE-DU-PU-RE TU-ME-I JA-SA-(?) U-NA-KA-NA-SI I-PI-(?)

Translation Process

Linear A :	ta -NU /	PA-E /	JA-NA-KI-TE-TE /	DU-PU-RE /	TU-ME-I /
Literal Text :	(contact)	(fathers)	(agitate - to make)	(purification)	(for - tomb)
Translation :	(contact)	(fathers) : (	stir to make)	(a purification)	(for tomb) :

No letter K in Latin. Substitute C or G. In this case the result is a G, based on probable parallel with Latin.

JA-SA /	sa - ra - me /	U-NA-KA /	NA-SI /	I-PI- na - ma /	si - ru - te
(by order)	(of duty - to)	(king)	(born)	(eponym)	(sire)
(by order)	(of duty to)	(the king)	(heir)	(who is named)	(sire)

Final Translation

(Contact) the fathers.

Stir to make a purification for the tomb, by order of duty to the king heir who is named sire.

KO Za 1

A-TA-I-*301-WA-JA TU-RU-SA DU-PU-RE I-DA-A U-NA-KA-NA-SI I-PI-NA-MA SI-RU-TE

Translation Process

> This word is often I-DA. The additional A at the end (I-DA-A) is necessitated by the absence of JA-SA-SA-RA-ME, the final syllable of which would have performed a similar function.

Linear A:	A-TA-I-*301 (NG_) /	WA-JA /	TU-RU-SA /	DU-PU-RE /	I-DA-A /
Literal Text:	(dip - to)	(wash)	(trouble)	(purification)	(for - gift / offering - to)
Translation:	(dip into)	(wash) :	(stir)	(a purification)	(for the offering to)

U-NA-KA /	NA-SI /	I-PI-NA-MA /	SI-RU-TE
(king)	(born)	(eponym)	(sire)
(the king)	(heir)	(who is named)	(sire)

Final Translation

Dip into the wash.

Stir a purification for the offering to the king heir who is named sire.

The King

Arch / Hook
(Arc)

— The arch is a shape which upholds a structure. (archi-tecture)

— The king (un-arc / mon-arch) functions as a structural support for society.

— The hook (unc / uncus) may be associated with the bent scepters known as crooks (frequently depicted in the hands of Egyptian pharaohs). Crooks are emblems of authority due to their use as tools for shepherding flocks. The Latin word implies hooking around the neck. Other Minoan images associate authority figures with leashes and the restraining of animals.

— The words anch-or, ang-le, and ank-le (L shaped joint) all relate to the idea of bending. In Latin, the word for snake (ang-uis) evokes a distinctive winding shape. Snakes are associated with kingship throughout much of the ancient world. They feature prominently in Minoan iconography. The words unc-tion and ung-uent relate to annointing and thus to kingship also.

— In Linear A, the words U-NA-RU-KA (un-arc) and U-NA-KA (unc) are both used in reference to the king.

While the restoration of this portrait is generally assumed to owe much to the imagination of Sir Arthur Evans, its link to language on recently deciphered artifacts merits consideration. Also noteworthy are the bent pins KN Zf 31 and ARKH Zf 9 which are associated with a high-priestess or goddess.

Ritual Bowl
TL Za 1

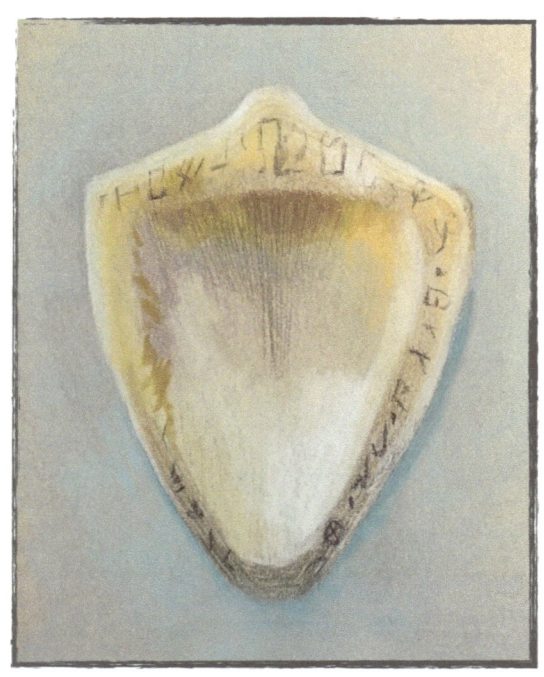

Heraklion Archeological Museum – HM 1545

TL Za 1

A-TA-I-*301-WA-JA O-SU-QA-RE JA-SA-SA-RA-ME U-NA-KA-NA-SI I-PI-NA-MA SI-RU-TE

Translation Process

Linear A :	A-TA-I-*301-^{NG} /	WA-JA /	O-SU-QA-RE /	JA-SA /	SA-RA-ME /
Literal Text :	(dip - to)	(wash)	(to soak - up)	(by order)	(of duty - to)
Translation :	(dip into)	(wash)	(to soak up) :	(by order)	(of duty to)

U-NA-KA / NA-SI / I-PI-NA-MA / SI-RU-TE
(king)   (born)   (eponym)   (sire)
(the king)   (heir)   (who is named)   (sire)

Final Translation

Dip into the wash to soak up, by order of duty to the king heir who is named sire.

Ritual Cup – Music & Dance
KN Zc 7

Minoan Dance Scene (clay sculpture)
Heraklion Archeological Museum

KN Zc 7

A-KA-NU-ZA-TI DU-RA-RE A-ZU-RA JA-SA-RA-A-NA-NE WI-PI

Translation Process

Syllable NE = possible affix. It perhaps functions similarly to the way that the syllable ME does in other instances:
JASA / SARA-ME (ME = of).
JASA / RAANA-NE (NE = of / having).

Linear A: A-KA-NU-ZA-TI / DU-RA-RE / A-ZU-RA / JA-SA / RA-A-NA-NE / WI-PI

Literal Text: (chant - to) (spaced intervals) (maintain) (with order) (run / move) (go back and forth)

Translation: (chant to) (rhythm) (maintain) (with order) (of movement to) (go back and forth)

Given the musical context (chanting and ordered movement back and forth), it seems likely that **spaced intervals** is a reference to measured time (rhythm). The next word, meaning to keep or maintain, supports this conclusion since together they form the ancient equivalent of "keep the beat".

Final Translation

Chant to maintain rhythm with ordered movement going back and forth.

Linear A	Latin : English
Linear A requires a vowel in this position. The Latin alphabet does not.	
A-KA-NU-ZA-TI	cantate : to chant or sing
DU-RA-RE	rarus : having intervals between [5]
A-ZU-RA	tuor : to keep or maintain
JA-SA	iussu : by order
(j = i)	Z becomes T in Latin.

Linear A	PIE : English
RA-A-NA-NE	rinea : to run [5] Proto-German : ren / rannjanan [5] Old English : rinnan [5]
WI-PI (VIB)	weip : to move back and forth [5] Latin : vibrare (move back and forth)

Ritual Dish
IO Za 6

Heraklion Archeological Museum – HM 3785

IO Za 6

TA-NA-I-*301-U-TI-NU I-NA-TA-I-ZU-DI-SI-KA JA-SA-SA-RA-ME

Translation Process

> The syllable ME = (of + to).
> If no word follows it, then ME = (of).
> See PR Za 1.

Linear A :	TA-NA-I-*301 (NG_)	U-TI-NU	I-NA	TA-I-ZU	DI-SI-KA	JA-SA	SA-RA-ME
Literal Text :	(strike)	(ringing noise)	(in)	(this)	(disc)	(by order)	(of - duty)
Translation :	(strike)	(a ringing noise)	(in)	(this)	(dish) :	(by order)	(of duty)

The root TIN is also found in the Latin word **tinnitus** (ringing noise). The sound being referred to here is probably the result of stirring in a cup or dish. Parallel roots for stirring are found on other ritual artifacts. This may be a clue to the Minoan fascination with spirals.

The words **disc** and **dish** are known to be etymologically related.

Final Translation

Strike a ringing noise in this dish, by order of duty.

Gold Ring
KN Zf 13

Heraklion Archeological Museum – HM 530

KN Zf 13

A-RE-NE-SI-DI-*301-PI-KE-PA-JA-TA-RI-SE-TE-RI-MU-A-JA-KU

Syllable *301 = NG + vowel. There are no word separations on this artifact. Syllable *301 could be an independent word or an affix, perhaps meaning something like the word **our**, based on the context.

Translation Process

Because there are no word separations on this artifact, the syllable A may belong in front of the word JA-KU rather than at the end of SE-TE-RI-MU. In either case, its purpose is probably to join the two words together. (stream + to / forth + wine) = wine-stream.

Linear A :	A-RE-NE-SI /	DI /	*301-PI-KE /	PA-JA-TA-RI /	SE-TE-RI-MU-A /	JA-KU
Literal Text :	(rinse)	(from)	(big)	(forefathers)	(stream)	(wine)
Translation :	(drink)	(from)	(great)	(forefathers)	(stream)	(of wine)

wine-stream

Final Translation

Drink from our great forefathers stream of wine.

Linear A	Latin : English
A-RE-NE-SI	recentiare : to refresh
DI	de : of or from
PA-JA-TA-RI	pater : father (**forefathers**)
JA-KU	iacchus : wine
(j = i)	

Linear A	Basque : English
A-RE-NE-SI	irentsi : to swallow [12] (i.e. to **rinse** down the throat)
*301-PI-KE	abiega : mighty or great [12] (**big**)
PA-JA-TA-RI	aitaren : fathers [12] (**forefathers**)
(j = i)	

Lamp Fragments
IO Za 5 and KE Zb 4

Minoan Lamp (similar to the inscribed fragments)
Sitia Archeological Museum – 3161

IO Za 5 / KE Zb 4

1. I-JA-RE-DI-JA I-JA-PA
2. JA-SI-E

Translation Process

		= to be
		= visibility

Linear A :   1.   I-JA   /   RE-DI-JA   /   I-JA   /   PA

Literal Text :   (to be for)   (radience)   (to be for)   (father)

Translation :   (to be for)   (light)   :   (for)   (father)

2.   JA   /   SI-E

(cause to)   (see)

(to)   (see)

These are the only Minoan lamps which contain text, making this parallel especially striking. The high incidence of synonyms and meaning which result from inserting word-breaks around JA and I-JA helps to identify these syllables as affixes on other artifacts as well.

I-JA	to be / to be for	IO Za 5 CR Zf 1 PR Za 1 KN Za 10
JA	cause to be / make it so / to make	KE Zb 4 IO Za 2 PK Za 8 PK Za 16 ZA Zb 34

Final Translations

1. To be for light, for father.
2. To see.

Offering Table
PK Za 16

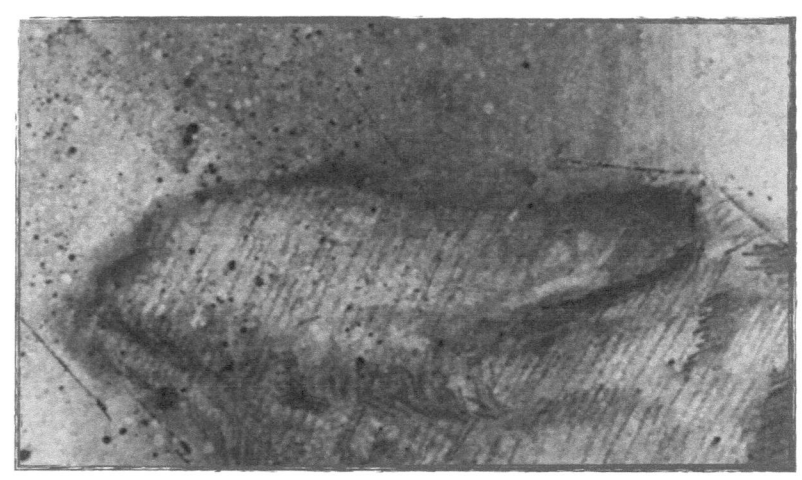

Ayios Nikolaos Archeological Museum–7231

PK Za 16

TO-SA PU-RE-JA

Translation Process

Linear A :   TO-SA   /   PU-RE   /   JA

Literal Text :   (burnt offering)   (pure   +   to make / cause to be)

Translation :   (burnt offering :   to make pure   )

Final Translation

To make pure a burnt offering.

Linear A	Latin : English	Linear A	Greek : English
TO-SA	tus : incense	TO-SA	thuos : burnt offering
PU-RE	purus : pure	(possibly ThuO-SA)	

Bone Label or Tool
ZA Zg 35

Sitia Archeological Museum—4632

ZA Zg 35

ME-MI-JA-RU SE-WA-AU-DE

Translation Process

		SEV		
Linear A :	ME-MI-JA-RU /	SE-WA /	AU /	DE
Literal Text :	(marrow - of to)	(sever / separate)	(away)	(from)
Translation :	(the marrow of to)	(separate out	)	

Prefix	Noun	Suffix	(ME) position-dependent result
	SA-RA	-ME	of duty + to
ME-	MI-JA-RU		marrow of + to

Final Translation

To separate out the marrow of.

Artifacts
PR Za 1 and KN Za 10

PR Za 1
Heraklion Archeological Museum – HM 2444

KN Za 10
Heraklion Archeological Museum – HM 2100

PR Za 1

TA-NA-SU-TE KE-SE-TO-I-JA A-SA-SA-RA-ME

Translation Process

The syllable ME = (of + to).
If no word follows it, then ME = (of).
See IO Za 6.

soot: *tkei: to settle or dwell [5]
that which settles [5]   sit, set, settle

Linear A :	TA-NA / SU-TE / KE-SE-TO / I-JA / A-SA / SA-RA-ME

kseti: to dwell, abide [5]

Literal Text : (contacting) (soot) (chest) (to be for) (by custom) (of - duty)

Translation : (contacting) (the soot) : (the chest is to be for) : (by custom) (of duty)

No letter K in Latin. Substitute C or G. In this case the result is a C, based on probable parallel with Latin.

Linear A requires a vowel in this position due to the natural limitations of its syllable system. The later Latin alphabet does not. (cista)

There may be a reason for the proximity and similarity of SU-TE and SE-TO on this artifact. **Soot** literally means that which settles, and KE / **SE-TO** (chest) is the object intended to hold the **set**-tled material, or **sed**-iment, possibly ashes of some kind. In view of the Proto-Indo-European and Sanskrit roots shown above, the initial K sound may be something similar to CH or TKH. This stands in contrast to the accepted etymology for the word chest, which is *kista.[6] Given the unmistakable shape of the artifact, it is possible that the etymology may be incomplete. It could also be that KE-SE-TO is a variant of *kista, perhaps a specific type.

TA-NA	(for) contacting	PR Za 1
TA-NU	(to) contact	KN Za 10 PK Za 8

Final Translation

The chest is for making contact with the soot, by custom of duty.

KN Za 10

TA-NU-MU-TI JA-SA-SA-RA-MA-NA DA-WA-(?) DU-WA-TO I-JA

Translation Process

The syllables MA and NA replace the usual ME. This peculiarity is probably required because ME would have inappropriately formed a link with the word after it.

Linear A :	TA-NU /	MU-TI /	JA-SA /	SA-RA-MA-NA /	DA-WA- e /	DU-WA-TO /	I-JA
Literal Text :	(contact)	(mud)	(by order)	(duty +?)	(offering-water)	(vat)	(to be for)
Translation :	(contact)	(the mud) :	(by order)	(of duty) :	(the vat is to be for the offering-water)		

The syllable DU is a prefix. This conclusion is based on the words DU/PURE and DU/RARE in PK Za 11 and KN Zc 7. In both instances DU causes the adjectives to become nouns.

TA-NA	(for) contacting	PR Za 1
TA-NU	(to) contact	KN Za 10 PK Za 8

Final Translation

Make contact with the mud, by order of duty. The vat is for the offering-bath.

KE-SE-TO / DU-WA-TO

The relationship between the words chest and vat as reflected in the parallel vocabulary of PR Za 1 and KN Za 10.

KE-SE-TO = **chest** = **ceseto** Latin: **cista** — cistern — **vat** **du/vato** prefix = DU-WA-TO

Linear A requires a vowel in this position due to the natural limitations of its syllable system. The later Latin alphabet does not.

No letter K in Latin. Substitute C or G. In this case the result is a C, based on probable parallel with Latin.

The syllable DU is a prefix. This conclusion is based on the words DU/PURE and DU/RARE in PK Za 11 and KN Zc 7. In both instances DU causes the adjectives to become nouns.

TA-NA	make CONTACT	TA-NU
SU-TE	soot / mud DIRT	MU-TI
KE-SE-TO	chest / vat CISTERN	DU-WA-TO
I-JA	is TO BE FOR	I-JA

Container Fragments
PE Zb 7 and PH Zb 5

Minoan Pithos (similar to the inscribed fragments)
National Archeological Museum – Athens

PE Zb 7 / PH Zb 5

1. A JA-WA-PI
2. WA-PI TI-NA-RA

Translation Process

				(VAP)
Linear A :	1.	A /	JA /	WA-PI
Literal Text :		(to / into)	(to make)	(vapor / spirit / alcohol)
Translation :		(	to make into spirit-alcohol	)

WAP / VAP
This word could also mean the opposite of what the root implies. If this is the case, then the word should be translated as **spirit-less** or **flat** wine (vappa in Latin).

2. WA-PI / TI-NA-RA

(vapor / spirit / alcohol) (container)

(spirit-alcohol container)

Final Translations

1. To make into spirit-alcohol.
2. Spirit-alcohol container.

Sea Goddess Artifacts
KO Zf 2, ARKH Zf 9, CR Zf 1, and KN Zf 31

Silver Hook or Pin KN Zf 31
Heraklion Archeological Museum – HM 540

KO Zf 2

A-RA-KO-KU-ZU-WA-SA-TO-MA-RO-AU-TA-DE-PO-NI-ZA

Translation Process

Linear A :	A-RA-KO	KU-ZU	WA-SA	TO	MA-RO	AU-TA	DE	PO-NI-ZA
Literal Text :	(keep)	(drip)	(water)	——	(sea)	(out)	(of)	(boat / deck of a ship)
Translation :	(keep)	(leaking)	(seawater)			(out)	(of)	(the boat)

Arceo (active) : I ward off. (I keep away).
Arceor (passive) : I am protected from.
Both forms are possible. See **spelling conventions** on page 82. Perhaps this inscribed bowl was intended as an offering to ensure good luck.

Final Translation

Keep leaking seawater out of the boat.

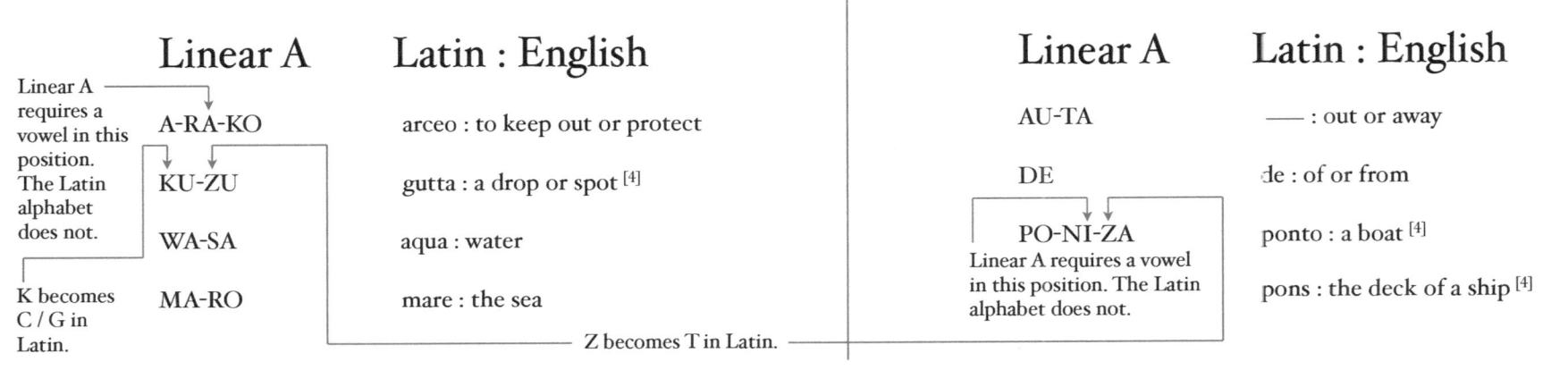

ARKH Zf 9 / CR Zf 1

1. JA-KI-SI-KI-NU MI-DA-MA-RA

2. A-MA-WA-SI KA-NI-JA-MI I-JA QA-KI-SE-NU-TI A-TA-DE

Translation Process

{ = to calm
  = the waves
{ = woman
  = of the sea

SI may be an ancient form of the word **the**.

Linear A :   1.   JA-KI-SI / KI-NU / MI-DA / MA-RA

Literal Text :   (flatten) (motion) (maid) (Mara / ocean)

Translation :   (flatten) (the waves) (mer - maid)

IAC : throw, cast, overthrow, flatten.[4]
Cast may be related, by parallel, to **spell-casting**.
See entry for the word magic – (QAK / HAG / HEC).

SE may be an ancient form of the word **the**.
(HEC)

2.   A-MA / WA-SI / KA-NI / JA-MI / I-JA / QA-KI-SE / NU-TI / A-TA-DE

(mother) (water) (foretold) (now) (to be) (hex) (nod / swaying) (today)

(foretell this now / in advance)

(mother) (of the water) : (to be foretold now) : (charm) (the waves) (today)

See various resources regarding the goddess Mami Wata. As mother of the water, she is associated with mermaids and snake-handling priestesses. Mermaids are often depicted combing their hair. These inscribed hairpins could have special significance, possibly equating the hair of the goddess with waves of the sea.

Heka : magic. Also the god of magic (Egyptian).
Hecate : goddess of magic (Greek).
Hagios : holy, magic, sacred (Greek).
Hagiography : writing about saints.
Hagiolatry : worship of saints.
Hag : witch, sorceress.
Hex : charm, curse or magical enchantment.

Final Translations

1. Flatten the waves mermaid.

2. Mother of the water, to be foretold now, charm the waves today.

KN Zf 31

SI SI-ZA-NE-*310 DA-DU-MI-NE QA-MI-*47-NA-RA A-WA-PI TE-SU-
DE-SE-KE-I A-DA-RA TI-DI-TE-QA-TI TA-SA-ZA TA-TE-I-KE-ZA-RE

Translation Process

Z becomes T in Latin.   Root words based on parallels with ARKH Zf 9 and CR Zf 1 (woman / sea).

(sita / nempe)   (domina)   (qua) (marina)

MPE   (VAP)

Linear A :   SI / SI-ZA-NE-*310 / DA-DU-MI-NE / QA-MI-*47-NA-RA / A-WA-PI / TE-SU /

(kwha)   See PE Zb 7 and PH Zb 5

Literal Text : (if) (permitted - truly) (from the - lady) (who is - mariner) (vapor / spirit - to) (these)

if / supposing

Translation : (if truly permitted) (from the lady) (who is of the sea) : (life to) (these)

(dare)   (TEG)

DE-SE-KE-I / A-DA-RA / TI-DI-TE-QA-TI / TA-SA-ZA / TA-TE-I-KE / ZA-RE

K becomes C / G in Latin.

These two words are not found in Latin. The letter Z functions as an S in both instances.

(discs - for) (to give - to) (is dedicated - to) (the - seas) (the - covering) (scar / sore / wound / offense)

in return for, to give

(islands for) (to give) : (is dedicated to) (the seas) (the transgression covering)

Compare with IO Za 6:
TA-I-ZU DI-SI-KA = this disc (circular dish).
TE-SU DE-SE-KE-I = these discs (circular islands). The choice of the word **islands** is based on the context of the sentence and the well-known geography of the region, which forms concentric circular islands. Disc, dish, and **desk** (table / surface) are known to be etymologically related.

Final Translation

Supposing it is truly permitted by the lady of the sea to give life to these islands in return,
the transgression covering is dedicated to the sea.

Observations

| | Dicite | Narrate | Cantate | Agitate |

1. Minoan imperatives are often closest to Latin present tense, second person, plural: A/DI-KI-TE, TA/NA-RA-TE, A/KA-NU-ZA-TI, JAN/A-KI-TE-TE. Notable singular imperatives are seen in the two etymologically related words JA-KI and QA-KI. Minoan syntax favors imperatives appearing first in the sentences or clauses they occur in, which typically represent instructions. As with many other words in Linear A, they are frequently affixed.

2. Affixes in Linear A are grammatically significant. They may even be serving some of the roles typically assigned to case or conjugation. The affixes ME and NE, for example, appear to be performing a rather genitive-like function, as can be reasonably inferred from various contexts. The affix A (to, into) is quite common. It is sometimes redundant to include it in the English translation process; in such instances it seems to function as an intensifying prefix. The affix I-JA / I-(JO) is also common. Grammatically, it acts as a demonstrative pronoun (this). (Proto-Italic: *eja/*ejo).[9] The Minoan sense of the word implies identification of purpose as well as a state of being in the **here** and **now**. It is probably a composite of two smaller units, which together literally mean "to be - for". The affix JA, without the preceding I, relates to **being** or **causing to be**. This is very likely related to the German word **ja** (yes, cause to be). Both I-JA and ME are position sensitive. In other words, a change in their position from suffix to prefix affects the grammatical role of the words they attach to. One of the most shocking aspects of Minoan affixes is that so many of them are recognizable to a modern English speaker: words such as **this** and **these**, **in** and **out**, as well as **the** and **do**.

3. Verbal noun DI-KI-TU. On artifact IO Za 2, a prefix change from the common A-DI-KI to JA-DI-KI impacts the verb's ending as follows: A-DI-KI-TE (verb) becomes JA-DI-KI-TU (verbal noun). This change of form is the result of different sentence structures. The latter requires a noun in order to make sense. In English, this can be illustrated with the examples **speak to** versus **speech make** (make a speech). The idea is that the verb becomes a noun to accommodate the change of affix. The remaining text on IO Za 2 is also a factor; it strengthens the need for a noun. Finding three synonymous Latin verbs in the imperative form (dicite, narrate, and cantate) in addition to appropriate usage of the verbal noun dictu is beyond the realm of chance. The corpus of text in Linear A is too small to suggest otherwise.

4. Spelling conventions. With the exception of diphthong notation, the spelling rules in Linear A are essentially the same as those in Linear B. Stated simply, final consonants are often omitted:[8] MA-TE = MA-TER / MI-DA = MaI-DAN. Some syllables may be aspirated:[8] TO-SA = ThuO-SA / PO-TO = BhO-ThO (both)–this word is found on clay accounting tablets where it refers to a tally of **both** sides of the document. Another important spelling rule is that an unpronounced vowel in one syllable may be signified by its repetition in another.[8] Ablaut and consonant mutation are also noted to play a role in Minoan spelling and word formation.

5. Etymologies. The word PI-TE-RI (father), on artifact PK Za 11, is closer to Sanskrit (pitar) than Latin (pater). Interestingly, its form seems to have survived in Latin through the name of the deity Jupiter (sky-father / heavenly-father). Another Minoan word with potential ties elsewhere is PA-JA-TA-RI which may be related to the Turkic word **pasha** (chief / leader). It is the word's context that suggests a connection. See artifact KN Zf 13. The pronunciation is also significant; this is not an isolated occurrence of the sign JA being linked with a SHA sound. WA-JA (Germanic wasche) is another example. The decipherment of Linear A may help clarify various etymologies (sarcina and cista); such was the case with Linear B.[8]

Summary

Minoan artifacts frequently have inscriptions that closely resemble one another. Their slight variations in spelling are correlated with specific synonym pairs found in European languages. The extent of these correlations is such that many of the inscriptions can now be deciphered. As a result, Minoan language is noted to be characteristically Italic, with a substantial Germanic component. Historically, it falls somewhere on the spectrum between Proto-Indo-European and Proto-Italic.

Significant progress has also been made in deciphering inscriptions which lack perfect parallels. This was achieved by the observance of secondary parallels in which synonymous vocabulary appears to be stated in a different order, or where general themes are discernable on artifacts of the same type. Many inscriptions either specifically label an object or identify its purpose. Crucially, it is the interconnectedness of vocabulary and affixes alike, through their recurring use in varying contexts and their correlations with later languages, that rules out chance as a possible explanation.

There are several factors which contributed to the longstanding challenge of deciphering Linear A. The inscriptions often contain compound words that are not immediately recognizable as such. Also, the vowels of root words do not always match those predicted by linguistic models. For example, the root NAM in Linear A is expected to have been NOM. This is shown to have a simple explanation: The sign NO does not exist in Linear A. Its sound was covered by the sign NA which served as a dual-syllable, and this phenomenon appears to have been common. In fact, the majority of O signs (NO, JO, DO, MO, QO, WO, and SO) were only developed later, with the arrival of Linear B. They would, therefore, all have required coverage by related signs in order for their sounds to have existed in Linear A. In some cases, vowel conflicts are attributable to issues of orthographic depth or to the uncertainty inherent in linguistic models. Another confounding factor has been that diphthong conventions in Linear A appear to differ from those found in Linear B. The Minoan preference was to indicate the second vowel of a diphthong rather than the first, and this practice may have extended beyond the traditional vowel pairings. The result is that while Linear A and B are undoubtedly related scripts, their subtle differences have likely been stumbling blocks to previous decipherment efforts. It is only through the application of consonant-parallels, which temporarily bypass vowels, that the necessary perspective can be gained to identify and resolve such orthographic conflicts.

References

1. Younger JG.
   Linear A texts & inscriptions in phonetic transcription & commentary
   (Internet). (First published 2000 Nov 30, last update 2020 Jan 2;
   last accessed 2020 Mar 3).
   http://people.ku.edu/~jyounger/LinearA/
   http://people.ku.edu/~jyounger/LinearA/misctexts.html
   http://people.ku.edu/~jyounger/LinearA/HTtexts.html

2. Godart L, Olivier JP. (GORILA)
   Paris (FR): Recueil des inscriptions en Lineaire A, vol. I–V (Etudes cretoises, 21);
   1976–1985. vol. I pp. (292–293). vol. IV pp. (8–9, 18–20, 24–27, 32–40, 42, 46–49, 58–59,
   72, 94, 112–113, 118–125, 146–147, 152–155, 158–159, 162). vol. V pp. (18–19, 22–27, 30–31).

3. Stevenson A, Lindberg CA, editors.
   New Oxford American dictionary (3rd edition)
   New York (NY): Oxford University Press; 2010.

4. Cassell's Latin and English dictionary
   Boston (MA) • New York (NY): Houghton Mifflin Harcourt Publishing Company;
   2002.

5. Harper D.
   Online etymology dictionary
   (Internet). (First published 2001; last accessed 2020 Mar 3).
   https://www.etymonline.com
   https://www.etymonline.com/word/dominate#etymonline_v_31785
   https://www.etymonline.com/word/in#etymonline_v_51323
   https://www.etymonline.com/word/municipal?ref=etymonline_crossreference
   https://www.etymonline.com/word/out#etymonline_v_9965
   https://www.etymonline.com/word/rare#etymonline_v_3371
   https://www.etymonline.com/word/soot#etymonline_v_23887
   https://www.etymonline.com/word/sore?ref=etymonline_crossreference
   #etymonline_v_23902
   https://www.etymonline.com/word/stream#etymonline_v_22161
   https://www.etymonline.com/word/*tkei-#etymonline_v_52709
   https://www.etymonline.com/word/*weip-?ref=etymonline_crossreference

6. TranCreative Software
   WordBook (version 5.1)
   TranCreative LLC; 2017.

7. Wikipedia
   G
   (Internet). (Page accessed 2019; last edited 2020 Apr 6).
   https://en.wikipedia.org/wiki/G

8. Chadwick J.
   The decipherment of Linear B (2nd edition)
   New York (NY): Cambridge University Press; 1958. pp. 75–76.

9. Wikipedia
   Proto-Italic language
   (Internet). (Page accessed 2019 Nov 25; last edited 2020 Apr 10).
   https://en.wikipedia.org/wiki/Proto-Italic_language

10. Wiktionary
    Reconstruction:Proto-Italic/jowos
    (Internet). (Page accessed 2019 Nov 25; last edited 2019 Dec 15).
    https://en.m.wiktionary.org/wiki/Reconstruction:Proto-Italic/jowos#Etymology
    Reconstruction:Proto-Indo-European/h₂ónkos
    (Internet). (Page accessed 2019 Nov 25; last edited 2019 Apr 12).
    https://en.m.wiktionary.org/wiki/Reconstruction:Proto-Indo-European/h₂ónkos

11. Strong J.
    New Strong's exhaustive concordance of the Bible
    Nashville (TN): Thomas Nelson Publishers; 1990. Strong's number G5015.

12. Google Translate
    (Internet). (Page accessed 2017; last accessed 2020 Apr 19).
    https://translate.google.com/#view=home&op=translate&sl=eu&tl=en&text=abiega
    https://translate.google.com/#view=home&op=translate&sl=eu&tl=en&text=aitar
    https://translate.google.com/#view=home&op=translate&sl=eu&tl=en&text=ama
    https://translate.google.com/#view=home&op=translate&sl=eu&tl=en&text=apaiz
    https://translate.google.com/#view=home&op=translate&sl=eu&tl=en&text=irentsi
    https://translate.google.com/#view=home&op=translate&sl=eu&tl=en&text=itsaso
    https://translate.google.com/#view=home&op=translate&sl=eu&tl=en&text=zauria

www.ingramcontent.com/pod-product-compliance
Lightning Source LLC
Chambersburg PA
CBHW041818080526

44587CB00004B/135